Looking *at* North Cornwall

by

Peter Davies

Published by
Bodmin Town Museum
Mount Folly, Bodmin, Cornwall, PL31 2HQ

About the Author

Peter Davies, born of Welsh parents, spent his childhood in the heart of rural south Northamptonshire before joining the Royal Air Force at seventeen. On leaving the RAF, his work eventually brought him to Bodmin in the late 1960's, and from September 1986 he began writing monthly articles for a local community magazine *'The Broadsheet'*, until March 1995. *'The Western Morning News'*, and various magazines, also published a series of articles. He was later invited to submit a regular feature for the *'North Cornwall Advertiser'* and to date over 90 monthly articles have been published. He has also been a contributor to local radio and TV stations.

In 1999 he became Chairman of the successful Bodmin Moor Project and in 2005/6 was project surveyor for the Blisland Commons Boundary Stones Scheme.

He was Chairman of Bodmin Town Museum for 18 years, has been President since 2004, and has a long history relating to various committees and bodies serving museums in the South West.

Through his great love of North Cornwall and its people, for many years he has been giving illustrated talks and leading guided walks regarding the region's rich history, its way of life, particularly that of the County Town of Bodmin, together with the heritage of Bodmin Moor.

Front cover image from centre top clockwise:
Temple Church, Delabole slate quarry, St Columb Major Church, Padstow, Bodmin Obelisk, Bedruthan Steps, Davidstow Church, Engine House Minions.

Published by:
Bodmin Town Museum, Mount Folly, Bodmin, Cornwall, PL31 2HQ.
Manuscript prepared for publication by W H & J M Johnson, the publishing team.

ISBN 978-0-9549913-8-8

Printed by MPG Books Ltd, Bodmin, Cornwall

Contents

*Dedicated to my wife Yvonne for her loyalty
and support, which have given me
confidence to continue with research and
writing over a period of twenty-five years.*

I would like to thank the following people and organisations:

Grace Cory, for all her help each month in ensuring articles and accompanying photographs were finished and ready for printing in the *'North Cornwall Advertiser'*. Maureen Tooze of Bodmin Town Museum, for access to the *'Cornish Guardian'* collection and permission to copy photographs. Dudley Prout, and Jim Edwards, *Launceston local historian*. The helpful staff at Bodmin Library. The Cornish studies Library, Redruth, for permission to use photographs from the *'Ellis Collection'* and the Copyright and collection holders including P J Garrett, G Starner, D Sandry, C Jenkin, K Keen, P Jewell, P Hodge and Grace Cory, who have allowed the use of their photographs. Bill and Janet Johnson, for their enthusiasm and many hours of committed hard work in bringing this book to fruition. Finally, thank you to those who have contributed information along the way.

Special thanks to Bodmin Town Museum colleagues for their warm friendship and continued belief in the success of the Museum.

P J C Davies, March, 2011

The Storm Clouds of War

THIS month we go back into those dark and desperate years of World War Two when the spirit of Cornwall and the rest of Britain were put to test once again.

In 1939 with the threat of war, increasing Air Raid Precautions were established with the HQ being situated in Bodmin Jail, air raid sirens were placed at the Police Station and the Gas Works in Berrycombe Road, new ambulances plus rescue equipment were also acquired and a successful appeal was made by the Fire Officer, C B Lyne, for more volunteers to increase the strength of the Auxiliary Fire Service.

In March of 1940 a full combined practice and demonstration was carried out. HEs (high explosive bombs) were assumed to have fallen in Cardell Yard, Crockwell Street and IBs (incendiary bombs) scattered over the area. Ambulances dealt with casualties while rescue parties and the fire brigade removed wreckage, rescued trapped persons and subdued the 'flames'. It would not be long before the valuable experience gained would be put to use.

For Bodmin Fire Brigade the special fire risks were identified and included the Gas Works, Petrol Depot Cardell Road, ARP Control Bodmin Jail, Victoria Barracks, GPO Mount Folly, Telephone Exchange Fore Street, GWR Station, S R Station, Bodmin Road (GWR) Station, aerodromes at St Eval, St Mawgan and St Merryn, ammunition dumps Glynn Valley, Respryn and Mount Charles, Beam Wireless Station at Lanivet, WRNS Glynn House, Saw Mills at Respryn and Bodmin Road.

From August of 1940 Germany did its best to crush the large cities and towns of Britain. For Plymouth, it was sheer hell with devastation on a large scale, never experienced before, forcing thousands of its population to flee each evening into the neighbouring countryside of Dartmoor or crowd the ferries and trains into Cornwall to escape the horror of what was happening, with many too fearful even to contemplate the fate of their houses or employment.

The forces of Hitler failed, but on those desperate nights of early 1941, when the glow in the sky and thud of the bombs could be seen and heard in Bodmin, the thoughts of Bodmin people must not only have been with their Plymouth cousins in their suffering but also with members of the Bodmin services engaged in help and rescue.

Censorship covered the activities of the fire brigade in the war, but from the clouds of obscurity a report was compiled of the blitz and inferno that the Brigade, many of whom were volunteers, attended. An inferno that, at its height, lit the countryside of Devon and Cornwall for miles around (indeed my wife's grandfather in Launceston was able to take a newspaper outside and read it such was the brightness of the sky) and people in St Germans woke one morning to find their gardens covered with burnt paper blown from the city.

1944 saw the D-Day storming of the Normandy Beaches at the start of the liberation of Europe. Spring of that year saw a visit to Cornwall of General Eisenhower and his military leaders, as the build up of forces was almost complete.

No one who lived in Cornwall at that time is ever likely to forget how crowded the harbours of the south coast were with the United States ships and how the whole country was a vast armed camp. D-Day was fast approaching, harbours like Dartmouth, Plymouth, Fowey and Falmouth were packed full of ships. Indeed, it was said at Fowey it was almost possible to walk from ship to ship across the harbour; then on 6th June they had almost completely gone, disappeared through the night, the emptiness was unreal.

With equally dramatic suddenness thousands of American troops left; they had 'occupied' Cornwall not as conquerors – as did the Germans in France – but as generous defenders who 'spent money like water' to the delight of the hotel managers and shopkeepers and with them, but more gradually, disappeared the miles of ammunition dumps which were piled beside many roads from Cornwall to the Midlands.

Probably few Bodmin people imagined the time might come when the Walker Lines would be transferred into an industrial estate. The supposedly temporary huts for soldiers built beyond the Barracks in the early months of the conflict were extended for the American troops thrust into the war by the Japanese at Pearl Harbour.

Cornwall gave hospitality to almost as many American servicemen as it does today to the holiday season visitors. The thinly populated stretch of the china clay country between Fraddon and Grampound Road was one enormous ammunition reserve, in dozens of clay dries and even the few people who lived there could only get to their homes by showing passes – at least until they were well known to the authorities.

Davidstow aerodrome was built for the American heavy bombers but no one asked the local people if it was a good idea to build an airfield on the north of Bodmin Moor and of course, the Moorland mists all too often rendered it unserviceable. It was virtually abandoned after D-day 1944.

Tales are still told of American armoured vehicles etc disappearing into the oblivion of Moorland bogs during manoeuvres; indeed if every tale was to be believed each marsh would be full to overflowing with American tanks. The embanked circular pools one finds on the east side of Brown Willy have much to do with tin workings but many are craters of shells which fell short of the hill target fired from an artillery range in the Cheesewring area of the village of Minions.

An aircraft came down in pitch darkness near the Cheesewring during the war, the two American pilots staggered out and supporting each other set off across the moor. Coming across a lonely farm house they banged on the door, enquiring whether the farmer could help, explaining they had just crashed their aircraft. "Oh no" they were told by the two farming sisters, "we never answer the door to strangers after dark". No amount of pleading would alter the situation and they were left to stagger on towards Kilmar no doubt wishing it was good old Kentucky.

Moorland came under the plough to meet the increased war effort. The Royal Cornwall Golf Course at Bodmin was given up to produce potatoes, sugar beet and cabbages. Woodland was cleared, a lot going for pit props needed in the mines and it was here that sometimes forgotten ladies in uniforms worked, the Women's Land Army – Timber Corps.

The Kendall Building at the former St Lawrence's Hospital became an emergency hospital. They received patients from the long ambulance trains (engines placed front and rear) that arrived in the evenings at Bodmin North station, at the end of a long and tiring rail journey from the south coast of England. Immediately transferred to a number of waiting ambulances outside the station they were taken to the hospital. Many soldiers had horrific injuries and owed their lives to the selfless dedication of doctors and nursing staff who had suddenly found themselves in a front line situation. The Royal Navy stored its rum in St Neot's slate quarry caverns, air raid shelters were built in back gardens and children tried on Mickey Mouse gas masks.

Today Bodmin's role has altered in world conflicts, for no longer will the town echo with the sound of the Light Infantry's boots at 140 steps to the minute and the shouted commands over military bands accompanying the quick marches to St Petroc's Parish Church.

But Bodmin will not be silent in its thoughts for Cornish men and women called upon, as in 1944, to serve their country. Our prayers go with them, just the same.

The Women's Land Army & Timber Corps.

The Women's Land Army was formed at the outbreak of World War II to work on the land, freeing the male workers to go to war. By 1943 there were some 80,000 young women working to feed the nation. They wore a uniform of green ties, green jumpers and brown felt slouch hats and worked from dawn to dusk each day, milking cows, digging ditches, sowing seeds and harvesting crops. **The Women's Timber Corps** worked to provide timber for the war effort, felling trees & sawing timber. The Women's Land Army was disbanded in 1950.

Recently, all surviving members of the WLA and the WTC received a special badge. This particular Badge was presented to the late Mrs. Eileen M. Orchard (née Shore) of Bodmin

(© *Mr. P. J. Garrett*)
Other images: George Ellis.
BTM (© Cornish Studies).

Loyal and Royal Stratton and Bodmin held the Key

CIVIL War began in Cornwall with the Launceston Assize of August 5th 1642 when the Royalists and the Parliamentarians put their case. The sheriff thereupon declared for the Royalists and proceeded to call up the County for the King. Once the all important harvest was over the Royalists and the Parliamentarians got down to the urgent business of competing for manpower, resources and boroughs of the county.

However, a number of boroughs, not under the fighting orders, remained for the most part neutral; the mayors adopting a wise course of entertaining whichever party happened to arrive on their doorstep. Thus, when Sir Richard Buller arrived in Bodmin expecting to meet his Parliamentarian force, he found Sir Ralph Hopton and the Royalists. A tricky situation indeed, but Sir Richard, being a prudent man, was not slow in finding a highway towards Launceston.

By the end of the year, Cornwall was held for the King; while across the River Tamar the Parliamentarians secured themselves in Plymouth under the governorship of John, second Lord Robartes, who had just completed the mansion on his Cornish estate, Lanhydrock.

In the New Year the Parliamentarians re-entered Cornwall to receive a bloody nose, at Braddock Down, near Boconnoc, Lostwithiel. Over 600 prisoners were marched to Bodmin to be impounded in Bodmin's old Friary Church. From then on both Bodmin and Launceston were barricaded against expected further Parliamentarian attacks.

The day of the famous battle for Stamford Hill, Stratton, May 15th, an all-important battle for Bodmin took place. The Earl of Stamford sent Sir George Chudleigh with 1,200 Parliamentarian men and horses to surprise the Sheriff who was reviewing the Royalist County Force behind the Bodmin barricades. Bodmin was really worth taking and defending, for behind the defences were the 600 prisoners and the Royalists' arms and ammunition. At one fearful stage all seemed lost when news came through of the great Royalist victory at Stamford Hill. This encouraged Bodmin folk from behind closed doors to join in with the King's cause, thus sending the Parliamentarians scuttling out over the Moor.

It was a costly time though, in manpower and money throughout Cornwall. For instance Bodmin's Mayor noted the cleaning and repairing the

Friary Church, guarding the prisoners there, burying those who died, entertaining leading Royalists and billeting soldiers – a very costly time for one and all.

War returned with a vengeance in 1644. The Earl of Essex arrived in the town in late July with the Parliamentarian army. However, within a month they were driven out; the vital Respryn Bridge over the River Fowey was secured. Bodmin's Mayor could bring out his best pewter again.

However, this could not continue and in 1646 General Fairfax, together with a very strong force encamped at Blisland. The Royalist House, who had watched his every move and advance from Cardinham Downs, made the prompt decision to evacuate Bodmin and head west. Bodmin stirred the following morning, swiftly realising it was now a Parliamentarian stronghold. The Mayor put away his best pewter again.

At Bodmin, General Fairfax received the surrender of Mount Edgcumbe from leading Royalists and the submission of Lord Mohun of Boconnoc. Within six months the Civil War in Cornwall was virtually over. Bodmin and Cornwall were exhausted.

The small hillside town of Stratton is half a mile from the famous Civil War battlefield site. The Royalist victory over the Parliamentary forces at Stamford Hill in 1643 is marked by a plaque at the Old Tree Inn, once the manor house of the Grenville family. The battlefield site itself, on the road to Poughill, has been sympathetically restored by local people, who have erected information boards explaining the significance of the site.

Civil War Artefacts (Bodmin Town Museum)

B61: 56oz. shot
(Found: Lostwithiel)

B647: 14 oz. shot
(Found: Stenalees)

B302: 56oz. shot
(Found: Bodmin)

B48: Spear or Pikehead (Found: Bodmin)

Camelford - A Trembling Hand and those 'Persistent Ladies'

ROTTEN Boroughs, dubious elections, partisan declarations, were all apparent at the time of the 1818 parliamentary elections and none more so than in Camelford, which reads like an 'Alice in Wonderland' story.

In 1818 there were 4 candidates for 2 seats: J Maitland and Mark Milbanke, who were nominees of Lord Darlington, opposed by Col Hanmer and J J Stewart, who were termed Independents. The Mayor, Matthew Pope, who was the returning officer, announced beforehand his intention of returning Lord Darlington's candidates and any elector who did not vote for them 'would find life rather unpleasant'. Amounts of £50, £90 and £100 (three instances) were distributed among the Darlington voters. In the result Maitland and Milbanke received 13 votes each and Hanmer and Stewart, only 10.

The latter raised a petition in the House of Commons, the hearing of which occupied no less than 12 days. The committee struck out two of the votes for the majority and admitted one, which had been refused by the Mayor for the minority thus making each side 11 votes. The election was declared void.

The charges of bribery were not dealt with at the hearing; had they been proved disfranchisement would have followed. *The Royal Cornwall Gazette* of April 17th 1819 makes the cynical comment 'As it would have defeated the purpose of both parties to have disenfranchised the borough, the charge of bribery was abandoned by mutual consent, an explicit avowal that both were equally criminal.' A writ was issued for a new election.

On the Election Day the town was thronged with people from the surrounding district and a number of special constables were sworn in. Proceedings began at 11am and Mark Milbanke asked for the 'bribery oath' to be administered to each voter as he came to the poll. This caused 'a momentary damp on the part of many of the electors – it is said that some of them took the Bible with a trembling hand!' The result was declared at 4 o'clock – Stewart and Allsop (who replaced Col Hanmer) 14; Milbanke and Maitland 12. It now seems a tremendous amount of bother over 26 votes.

Camelford was not alone in the election shenanigans. If anything, the following was even more blatant. The result of the poll of 1703 to elect

2 members for Lostwithiel was: Francis Robartes (Tory) 20; Russell Robartes (Tory) 17; James Kendall (Whig) 5; Joseph Addison (Whig) 4. The Returning Officer, then the Mayor of Lostwithiel, was an ardent Whig and declared Kendall and Addison duly elected! The Robartes brothers brought 3 petitions against them, the third succeeded and they were unseated.

One hundred years ago, in January 1910, a political meeting was arranged to be held in Bodmin's Market House, at which the principle speaker was to be the Right Honourable Member for Dundee, Mr Winston Churchill, who was then a young Cabinet minister.   The meeting was organised by the Liberal Association, for Mr Churchill had joined the ranks of that party.

Doors were to be opened at 6pm, but earlier there had been rumours that a band of suffragettes were in town, so a thorough search of the building was undertaken in the late afternoon in order, as the local press stated, 'to obviate any unseemly behaviour on the part of these persistent ladies'.

Bodmin Museum Celebrates

FOR Bodmin Town Museum, the 2009 season gave a reason for celebration as the number of visitors passed 10,000; in fact there were 10,479. This achievement, together with glowing compliments given verbally or written in the visitors' book, has given us a great deal of satisfaction. The visitors' book, which is always open for inspection at the reception desk, makes interesting reading. Apart from the geographic spread of visitors from across the globe, it is the comments that so frequently express an appreciation of having a museum full of local history and displayed in such a manner to make a visit enjoyable and worthwhile.

The museum is proud that the hard work and selfless dedication of the museum curator, Mrs Maureen Tooze, has been recognised after a long journey of 25 years. I personally cannot think of any task that Maureen has undertaken without success, much enthusiasm and tremendous dedication to detail.   In recognition of her outstanding work, Maureen was awarded a prestigious citizenship award at the inaugural 'Cornwall Celebrates Volunteers' event that sadly Maureen, through illness at the time, could not attend but was ably represented by her husband, Brian. Maureen, who was the first winner of Cornwall Celebrates Culture category, also received a rare Citizenship Award presented by the Town Mayor at the annual museum lunch.

Cliff and Me ....Mrs Thatcher Makes Three!

FROM August 1940 Germany did its best to crush the cities and morale of the British people. Through this article let us reflect on life in Cornwall during one week of October 1940, when life would still have to go on despite the restrictions, and efforts would be made to ensure it would be business as usual in Cornwall. For example the Bodmin Moor Commoners Association advertised their AGM, Church and Chapel continued regular services and Sunday was still looked upon as a quiet day. Weekdays, the shops managed to serve supplies despite rationing of goods and people queued with as much patience as possible. Parish Councils still debated at meetings and carnival queens and attendants were elected for the coming twelve months. Delabole saw the Boys' Brigade on parade and marching through the village as usual. The Women's Institute tried variations of wartime recipes. St John Ambulance first aid training seemed more important than before and school children rehearsed air raid drill that included marching in single file to the air raid shelters.

Mrs W Trenouth of Tresallyn Farm, St Merryn, reported she was picking strawberries in her garden and all were of good quality.

Residents of Bodmin were advised of an additional filter to guard the public against what was known as arsenical smoke gas and informed it was extremely important these filters were fitted to the respirators which had already been supplied to them. It was announced that babies' protective helmets would also be fitted on a date to be advised.

For a number of months the town of Wadebridge used a ship's siren as an air raid alarm but this was found to be rather ineffective and was to be replaced by a new siren situated on top of the Town hall roof to give a more reliable service for the town outskirts and surrounding parishes.

A debate was taking place "Will the Old Cornwall Society with the word 'Old' deleted from its title mean quite the same thing?" The meeting decided to refer the matter to the next AGM. I think the question is still being debated even now.

The subject of acorn feeding to cattle and pigs was raised due to the reduced supplies of meal available. A Ministry leaflet was issued 'Grow More' but was very cautious by recommending a gradual introduction over a period of 77 days and 'they should fatten well on 14 and a half pounds of mangolds and 7oz of fish meal'. It was said acorn fed pigs yielded excellent hard bacon.

'Put that light out!', Chief Warden Hodges of Dad's Army fame would have had a field day at St Austell Petty Sessions. The accused stated that the light showing from a room occupied by him was so mysterious that he and PC Hugo spent some time investigating where it came from. They eventually came to the conclusion that it was reflected up from a heavy dark carpet, under the bottom of the perfectly fitting black out curtains and out through the top of the window, although the window was also covered by a pelmet. An involved explanation, but any light showing was a serious offence and resulted in a fine of 10 shil-lings (50p). Other lighting offences dealt with a cyclist with too bright a front lamp (it should have had a shade); a bonfire on an allotment glowing at night and 2 fields of stubble that blazed up during the black out.

A gentleman from Portscatho was fined for parking his car in Church Street, St Austell, on the wrong side of the road after dark for more than two and a half hours, on returning at 11.20pm he was apprehended by the police. He told magistrates that he had been on sick leave, but was called to a Home Guard meeting and expected the meeting to last about 20 minutes – instead it lasted more like 7 hours!

At the Trigg sessions the landlords of the New Inn, St Breward and the inn at Blisland were both fined due to light coming from a window. The magistrate issued a severe lecture as to the seriousness of the offence in wartime Britain with the enemy planes on bombing missions at night.

This has been a snapshot of a week in Cornwall 70 years ago, during the week in which I was born. As for Mrs Thatcher, the 'Blessed Margaret' shares the same birth date, October 13th. You may ask, what of Cliff Richard? Well, he was born around 12 hours later than me (October 14th in India) no doubt bouncing around the bed singing "Congratulations and Celebrations!"

North Cornwall's Little Train Robbery!

IF you ever wished to accomplish the perfect crime, the following is surely not the way to do it - more 'Carry On' than 'Carry Off'.

In the summer of 1974, four men, all from the Kirkby area of Liverpool, drove to Cornwall where they stayed overnight with a local postman and his wife in Bodmin, with whom one of them lodged. Unbeknown to the postman, they had hatched a plan to rob the mail train at Bodmin Road station.

Following an evening spent drinking heavily the four men arrived at Bodmin Road station early in the morning intent on carrying out their plan but they arrived an hour too soon and robbed the wrong train!

A railway man, Mr John Vanderwolfe of Bodmin, described how early in the morning of July 4th, he was sorting the parcel mail bags which had been dropped off from the parcels train (not the mail train) on the platform, when he saw two men walking towards him. "At first I thought they were just people coming early as they sometimes do, to catch the train," he said. The next thing he knew was when the men, who by then were wearing balaclavas, stood next to him. They made him lie down, tied his hands with cord, bound his legs with sticky tape and placed a hessian sack over his head.

They asked John where the registered letters were and he replied that he didn't know. One of the men said, "I am only going to ask you once," and again John replied that he didn't know. Mr Vanderwolfe said that he heard one of the men say, "He is not going to give us any trouble; he is more frightened than anything".

When he heard a car rev up he thought the men had gone. He then managed to get one of his hands free, pulled the sack from his head and crawled to the signal box to raise the alarm.

Three of the men made their escape to Plymouth where they were stopped on the Tamar Bridge. The fourth returned to his Bodmin lodgings. Amongst the three passengers was Paul Conteh, the younger brother of the then world light-weight boxing champion, John Conteh. Police Constable Bryan Hannaford, who had stopped the car, could not smell any alcohol on the men's breath. On further examination a number of boxes were revealed in the boot containing plates commemorating the wedding of Princess Anne and Captain Mark Phillips which made the policeman suspicious. All three men were taken in separate police cars to Liskeard Police Station. Detective Superintendent William Willmott, who interviewed the men, told the jury that all three men said they were going to Plymouth on business and had no knowledge about a 'Bodmin Road job.'

During the trial a blood-stained shirt, with a small cut on it, was produced in evidence; the blood was group A, the same as one of the robbers, and also the same as blood found on a number of mail bags the forensic expert had examined. The prosecution claimed that the cut on the shirt was made by the same knife which was used to cut open the mail parcel bags.

The jury took half-an-hour to reach a unanimous verdict of 'guilty' following the eight-day trial, and the sentences given ranged from three to five years.

The judge, Mr Justice Cantley, addressed John Brown, who with his brother, was said to have instigated the conspiracy, "You have abused the hospitality of the people in Bodmin, who took you in as a lodger, and you must have told your brother of the opportunity there was for a train robbery in Bodmin."

John Vanderwolfe was awarded £25 from public funds for his quick-wittedness in raising the alarm, and identifying the miscreants. Mr Justice Cantley stated, "I was impressed, not only with your evidence, but also the way you acted in the circumstances in which you were placed. Your prompt action and cool-headedness in the situation contributed to the apprehension of these criminals".

As for John Brown, Mr Ian Black QC said, "What a way to plan a great train robbery - you get the wrong train and you get the wrong time of the train you want and you start out by having a monumental party and advertise your presence. Does it make sense? I ask you to say it does not."

The hero, that fateful morning, John Vanderwolfe, the young 19-year-old railway man is, I am advised, the current Town Clerk to Tiverton Town Council. He is also the son of former Mayor of Bodmin, Cllr Harold Vanderwolfe.

Today, the signal box is a popular café and the mail train that arrived on time after the criminals had left is sadly no more, our post being transported by road or air.

The Hand of God Moved in Mysterious Ways in St Columb

CHINA is the third largest country in the world, the nation with the greatest population and has the oldest continuous civilisation of any country. It can claim many inventions including paper, printing, ink, silk, porcelain, stained glass, fireworks and gun powder.

In this country gun powder is the oldest of all explosive mixtures for different intended uses, much in demand in Cornwall in the early days of deep mining and quarries. Although, in 1605, along came Guy Fawkes with an attempted different use, that of blowing up the Houses of Parliament, King James I and his ministers. Barrels of gun powder were stored in vaults underneath Parliament, but the plot was exposed and since that time the date serves to perpetuate the ancient custom of burning the effigy of Fawkes.

An explosion did take place in St Columb but the outcome was surely not what was intended. In the 17th century a parish might be likened to a general business, managed by parish officers. It had stores of cattle and goods, it lent money – at interest of course for the benefit of and to the inhabitants – and has charge of what may be termed civil defence or the home guard armoury. In 1676 the 'stock' of St Columb holdings included gun powder, which was stored in the church.

Hal, the historian of that period, records that the greater part of the church of St Columb was casually blown up with gun powder, by three youths of the town. He goes on to advise *'they were scholars, who, in the absence of their master and the rest of their companions, ignorantly set fire to a barrel of gun powder that with the parish stores, laid up in the stone stairs of walls of the rood-loft or choir gallery'.* That gives us the information that the parish had a stock of gun powder, presumably for mining purposes, but also exactly where it was stored. We have also learned that the church was used as a schoolhouse.

The damage done was considerable. The cost of repairs amounted to £350.00; today perhaps nearer a six figure sum. Hal further reports *'the glass windows, roofs, timbers, stones and pillars, made a direful concussion together to the defacing of the front of the church and many pews thereof '.*

There were freakish results and escapes. Nicholas Jane, a hellier (slater), was on a ladder working on the roof when the explosion took place; both he and the ladder were thrown to the ground without damage. The church bible and common prayer book, with their leaves open in the rector's pew, scarcely two feet from the rood-loft, were neither singed, moved or damaged in any way. Not so much as any dust about them, though any stones were cast about the church. The communion table, which was very old, was spared and preserved in a likewise manner, when the very walls and pillars near to it were shattered.

Bodmin Jail was made of sterner stuff. Following its sale in the late 1920s the slates, timbers etc from its roofs and floors were removed, but when it came to the granite stone walls, the demolition was not a success; the lime mortar had fused with the granite stone and the use of explosives proved to be impracticable.

To visit Trago Mills, the well known shopping complex, alongside the A38 road through the Glynn Valley between Bodmin and Liskeard, it is hard to visualise it being the site of a gun powder factory and a great explosion in July 1865. The report tells all '*The grinding mill at the Trago Powder Mills, in the parish of Broadoak, blew up on Wednesday afternoon, at about four o'clock. The mill contained about one ton of powder. Luckily there were no men in the mill at the time, but there were two men in the cooper's shop about eighty yards distant, who escaped unhurt. The roof of the mill was completely blown off and the end wall blown down. The explosion was heard at Liskeard, a distance of five miles, and throughout the surrounding neighbourhood. The mills were worked by the Herodsfoot Powder Company.*' The manufacturer of gun powder would always be a dangerous occupation and explosions were not unknown and in an attempt to mitigate the damage and danger, trees were always planted to create a damp atmosphere and break the force of an explosion.

'Fireworks'

©*WHJ/GS*

Hunter Gatherers - Flint Stones at Castle Canyke

HOW far back can we journey to come across the first human activities in or around Bodmin, the centre of Cornwall? The answer - quite a long way really; in fact it was the Mesolithic Period (8500-4000 BC). The ice age was retreating as temperatures rose and hunter gatherers, who visited Britain from mainland Europe found rising sea levels were making Britain the island we know today, and from that period in our history the British race evolved. We are aware of their presence to the east of Bodmin at Castle Canyke hill fort where flint was found and at Treffry, when excavations were being undertaken in 1971 for the A30 Bodmin by-pass.

At that period in our history the early hunters would have experienced a far different landscape than that of today, the higher hills would have been heathland with scattered birch woodland in the lower valleys. Change gradually took place with oak and hazel becoming predominant, and within 1,000 years most of Cornwall was covered in dense forest. No trace remains of those early people; their life was transient, moving with the seasons, only the worked flint used as barbs on arrows and spears give us clues as to where our ancestors set up their seasonal camp.

The Middle Bronze Age, around 1800 BC, left us with tangible remains as they settled and farmed, taking in land and gradually clearing the woodland to create stone hedged fields for growing crops and pasture land for the livestock. They built round houses and settled communally in which these days would be regarded as a hamlet. Today, a great deal of evidence still remains on Bodmin Moor. It was a time when burial barrows were built with earth and stone, usually in a prominent place. Archaeologists made mention of barrows, including a cist (pronounced 'kist' – a stone lined chamber) in fields adjoining Bodmin Common Beacon, and a survey carried out in 2007, revealed the remains of one possible barrow site. The fields now occupy an area once known as Bodmin Downs and were used for rough grazing until they were enclosed and later ploughed. This could well be the logical reason for the barrow's disappearance after the 1850s enclosure.

Entering what is known as the Iron Age, we have the largest Iron Age fort in Cornwall, namely Castle Canyke, which covers 18 acres in a very commanding position to the east of Bodmin. In 1813 the fort was in open moorland but by 1849 it had been enclosed by a Cornish hedge which still surrounds the site today. Regrettably the interior was sub-divided into four fields by further hedges, plus the building, albeit of a very attractive barn, at the highest point in the centre of the site. If this had not happened the overall effect of entering the site today would be quite dramatic and the reason behind it most obvious with the land dropping away westwards towards the River Camel valley and to the south the high range of hills facing Bodmin. Its effectiveness was not lost in later history when used as an assembly point for the Cornish Rising against Henry VII's Scottish Subsidy in 1497, with a subsequent march led by Thomas Flamank of Bodmin and Michael Joseph An Gof to the Battle at Blackheath.

Castle Canyke Iron Age Fort as it is today.

In 1549 Perkin Warbeck, who claimed to be the younger son of Edward IV and considered to be Pretender to the throne, gathered supporters to his cause at Castle Canyke and marched off to yet another bloody end. Bodmin was in Royalist hands for most of the Civil War. There was skirmishing in the vicinity during 1643, changing hands briefly in 1644 but quickly retaken for the king, before finally falling to Cromwell's troops in 1646, shortly before the end of the hostilities. Cannon balls have been found within Castle Canyke and the immediate area and it is known that troops occupied the fort at this period in time. Today, the site is one of two Iron Age forts owned by Cornwall Council; the other being the magnificent Warbstow Bury.

Finally, in our journey of early settlements we go to the Roman age and Nanstallon, where the remains of a Roman fort, the only one so far that can be firmly identified, was excavated and shown to be occupied for thirty years in the second half of the first century AD. It probably had a dual role high on the hill overlooking the then highest navigable point on the River Camel and protecting its mineral operations within the area, together with an important ford. All in all it was very strategically sited. The fort was known as Tregear and derives its name from Cornish words *'tre'* meaning farmstead and *'ker'* meaning fort. Authorised archaeological excavations have taken place and although not large, it included barracks and officers' quarters and was defended by double wooden gates, angle towers, turf ramparts and a surrounding ditch. Formidable enough to repel any local skirmishing and of course the Romans provided the basis of the excellent road network that Nanstallon is fortunate to have today.

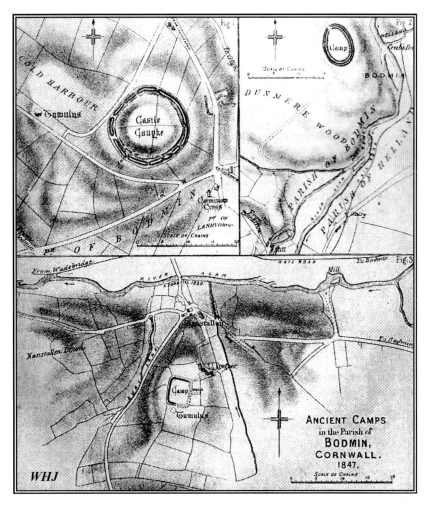

Mayor Horace Kinsman holds aloft a triumphant 13 year old Denis Cooper, who had arrived at the Turret Clock, clasping the silver ball, in 1946. The completion of 'Beating the Bounds'.

'Beating the Bounds'
Ellis Images from Bodmin Town Museum (©Cornish Studies Library)

Beating the Bounds - muddy but fun

"OYEZ! Oyez! Oyez! Thus far extends the ancient Borough of Bodmin. Oller, Boys, Oller!". Very few of the residents of Bodmin over the years have not participated in the old ceremony of 'beating the bounds' and responding to the Town Crier's shout of "Oller, Boys, Oller".

In April 1934 the ceremony was revived after 11 years and the town held a high holiday; the children were freed from school and most of the shops were closed. This led to a large crowd being assembled at the west end of the town to await the hospital clock striking nine; then, at the appointed time the Municipal Band, at the word from their leader, Mr W T Lobb, struck up the lilting 'Bodmin Riding' and amid much cheering the cavalcade, headed by the Mayor and Town Crier, both on horseback, headed off through the town in the direction of Callywith Gate. In previous years the turnpike gate was astride, what is today, the A30 road to Launceston, when you would have paid a toll to continue your journey.

In the streets of Bodmin, the jovial Town Crier, Mr Stanley Morris, had thrown scores of brightly polished pennies for the children to scramble about, but the walkers pushed on with determination knowing they had 18 miles to go over rough country. The three men deputed to 'beat the bounds' were Robert Bray, Dick Dymond and Nick Rosevear. From Callywith they passed through Margate Wood, named after the saint 'Margaret' who had an ancient chapel in the neighbourhood. An unfortunate incident took place as the horsemen were crossing a stretch of treacherous bog land. The Town Crier negotiated a wire fence, when the horse of the Borough Surveyor, Mr R T Buscombe, who was following him, suddenly reared and threw its rider. Fortunately the ground was soft and Mr Buscombe escaped with nothing worse than a muddy coat, bruising and a red face.

At Fletchers Bridge, in the time honoured fashion, the Crier threw pennies into the river, from where the route to Carminnow Cross took one over or through a narrow water tunnel under the railway line (not allowed today). The cross has been re-sited to the centre of the A38 roundabout, but in those days stood at the junction of the Liskeard and Lanhydrock roads. Incidentally, the fields passed through on the approach to the A38, known as Turfdown, are thought to have originated from a large unenclosed common where the people of Bodmin used to take turf as fuel. Turf Street, in the town, probably took its name as being a place where turf was stacked or turf cutters lived.

Onwards to Halgavor Moor, which means 'Goat's Moor' where, centuries ago, local people pastured their goats. It was also a rendezvous for the youngsters of Bodmin to play a game where they elected a judge and held mock trials, with their prisoners being committed to the 'Dragon's Pits', which at the time were being filled with the town's debris. Today, it is the site of the popular Dragon Leisure Centre and housing.

A halt at Blowing House for refreshments which consisted of some 9 gallons of beer, nearly 300 bottles of minerals, over 1,000 buns and 600 pasties. Pennies were again thrown in the river for the children and a well-earned rest was taken for an hour. Blowing House was so named due to the process of tin smelting which was believed to have taken place in the vicinity, with waterpower being used. A former mill leat serving Laveddon and St Lawrence's corn mills also runs from this point.

The next step was to follow the river to Dunmere and take Tanwood Lane to Scarletts Well. Over the centuries people flocked to this well in the hope of a cure by the alleged medicinal properties of the water; at one time becoming so popular that the militia were needed to keep order. There followed an uphill trek past Bodiniel, once an important manor, to Penbugle Farm, a short rest taken for refreshments and finally on to the Salting Pool, thereby completing the beating of the bounds.

The Mayor, Mr Cecil Lyne, had two more duties to perform. First to throw the silver ball into the pool for the hurling to take place, then go back into the town to be at the Turret Clock to receive the silver ball from the lucky youngster whose reward was 15 shillings (75p today).

Many of us have treasured memories of 'beating the bounds', such as losing our wellies in that muddy field at Fletchers Bridge or falling into a stream, the satisfaction of beer and pasties at Blowinghouse or catching new pennies in the river.

An ancient tradition of long standing, which hopefully will be kept in being for future generations to experience, to learn the boundaries of the parish and of course "Oller, Boys, Oller".

"As we enter 1969 we have to mention the weather"

IN the days before 'Climate Change or Global Warming' influenced the news, weather was just weather, it had its extremes, always appeared to rain at the most inconvenient times, or the weather was too hot, too dry, always a topic of conversation.

1968 was quite a dry year, nowhere more so than Bude, but for Camelford, December would be very soggy with rain falling 23 days of the month, culminating on Christmas Eve with 2.45 inches of, equal to 252 tons of rain. This led to flooding of houses and business properties. Not a pleasant Christmas for a number of people affected. It had brought back memories of a few years previous of what came to be called 'The Great Storm of Camelford'. The day was 8th June 1957, and on that day 'Flaming June' it was not. An amazing deluge of tropical proportions descended on Camelford and the immediate area bringing 8 inches of rain in 24 hours; of this a total of 6.34 inches fell in two and a half hours between 12.30pm and 3.00pm. It was recorded at that time as the thirteenth heaviest rainfall in the British Isles during the previous 100 years.

To put it in context, the Lynton and Lynmouth disaster on 15th August 1952 received 9 inches in about 7 hours and during the Boscastle Flood on 16th August 2004 in a 24 hour period Otterham received nearly 8 inches and Lesneweth 7 inches of rain.

Leaving 1968, Bodmin was next to experience the extremes of weather. The local paper reported on 23rd January 1969 'A Hurricane Tears through Bodmin'. In a few terrifying minutes daylight turned to darkness, broken only by flashes of lightning, claps of thunder and hailstones whitening the streets. Then came the wind roaring in at over seventy miles an hour; damaging houses, leaving bungalows along Beacon Road with badly damaged roofs and Bosvenna Hotel in Priory Road left with structural damage. Over 200 trees were uprooted in the Glynn Valley as it sliced through the forestry.

Mid February brought more adverse weather news; the sea froze on beaches, icicles hung from cliffs and Cornwall suffered the heaviest snowfall in years with 80 miles per hour gales and temperatures plunging to 17 degrees. Two members of the jury were flown by helicopter to attend the hearing of a case at Bodmin Assizes. They had managed to get from Kilkhampton to Bude by road, but no further because of the snow. A helicopter was scrambled from RAF Chivenor to collect them and they landed on the football pitch, Priory Park, Bodmin to be hurried across to the Assize Court.

Entering 1969 the papers reported a storm over rail fares, floods followed the wettest Christmas, John Pardoe MP for North Cornwall stated housing waiting lists were too long and Christmas mail was only slightly down on previous years. The total figures at the postal sorting office in Bodmin from 13th December to Christmas Eve inclusive, reached half a million. The rail fuss, by the way, was a proposal to raise fares by a supplement of £1 during the summer period on return popular trains. Not a good start to 1969 for British Rail when the Plymouth rail manager suggested that, "If the line is singled from Plymouth to Penzance, trains would be faster" – all to do with less sharp bends you see. However, Cornwall was not convinced that it was a very good idea and County Hall got very excited in their opposition, no doubt fearing branch line status for the main line.

The first breathalyser case was heard in Bodmin when a licensee was fined and banned for one year. The licensee failed to negotiate the Finn VC Estate junction and collided with a wall.

Headlines stated 'Prospecting for Tin in Cornwall' production soon is company's hope. Last year in 1968 Cornwall produced tin worth £2 million pounds, about one ninth of tin used in Great Britain. Canadian firm Prado Exploration Ltd will shortly start exploratory work, Wellington Mine, Carnon Downs.

The first week in February saw the opening of the *'Drum Major'* after refurbishment of the former regimental hospital. Saltash born, Mr Ken Allen, proprietor and licensee was keen to keep a link with the DCLI (Duke of Cornwall Light Infantry) for example 'The Lucknow Lounge, the Paardeberg Hall, the Gaza Restaurant and even the Punjab Kitchen'. Today the building is the 'Eclipse Night Club'.

At the first meeting of Bodmin Borough Council, the Town Clerk reported on a meeting in London with the developers, Ministry of Housing and Local Government and the Greater London Council concerning the move to Bodmin by Flann Microwave and Microtest Ltd. A letter from the Ministry stated that loan sanction would be given for these two firms. The GLC had confirmed that housing advances would be available to employees moving with these companies for properties in Bodmin.

In February 1969 Mr Peter Bessell, MP for the Bodmin Constituency opened the factory of Drayton Engraving and Nameplate Co. on the then new Walker Lines Industrial Estate; employing 30 people, he stated the firm's activities would make available above £500 per week for spending in Bodmin.

In March the police advised they would step up the fight against drug trafficking – large quantities were being smuggled into holiday areas.

By April, Bodmin Jail was under threat, the headline ran 'Bodmin Jail Gatehouse for Export. Americans Probably Keen to Purchase'. "We intend to put advertisements in American newspapers, and probably tie it up with Mayflower year", stated the managing director, whose company had just bought the prison. On the 10th November, the same year, English Heritage listed Bodmin Jail, including the Gatehouse.

St Lawrence's Hospital advised opportunities for students and pupils in psychiatric nursing, salary starting at 18 years, £495 pa.

On the entertainment front the popular rock group 'The Gin House' travelled down to Redruth for the finals of the Cornwall Open Talent Competition and carried off the winners' trophy. No surprise there for a very talented group.

While at Bodmin Jail, the members were being entertained by Paul Daniels, Vince Eager, Mai Loo and Farina.

Publishers Comment:

We can confirm the author's comments on the weather in 1969. We travelled down to Cornwall in late February for our marriage. Several of our guests did not make it through the snow on Bodmin Moor!

**Bodmin Fire Brigade 1930: same people, same machine, same place
– different hats!**

Serious fire at St Lawrence's Hospital - Padstow ready to launch lifeboat - why?

IN this article we look back over the history of Bodmin's Fire Brigade. The town museum houses Bodmin's first fire engine (The Manual Pump) believed to have been acquired on or about 1770 and manned by anyone who was available at the time required.

One hundred years later this was no longer thought to be satisfactory and an official band of fire fighters was formed. The following year the mayor of the town, Mr Joseph Stevens, convened a meeting on 10th December 1872 and the 'Bodmin Volunteer Fire Brigade' came into being, with three engines and a rate of pay of 9d per hour.

One year passed before action was seen at 10.30pm on 21st December 1872 at the stables of Mr Simon Hugo in Castle Street. They were kept busy until 2am the following morning. Nine years later saw the brigade tackling the huge fire that destroyed a considerable portion of Lanhydrock House, so similar to the fire that raged with great violence in 1819 and burnt down Glyn House. On both occasions the inhabitants of Bodmin were raised from their beds by the bugles and fire bells 'and repaired with great haste to the spot' though in truth, little could be done.

It was not all tragedy of course, humour shines through like the following entry taken direct from the log book of 1898: *Friday 1 April 1898. Drill. Hydrant tried Rhind Street and Castle Street, Honey Street and hydrant outside Mr Tonkin's shop in Fore Street and the hose bursted and drowned Mr Sangwin's shop and spoiled a lot of goods in his shop and Mr Sangwin was greatly annoyed. Members present: Capt Bawden, W Shelley, N Climo, Perry, F Weary, C Weary; Henderson was to the hydrant and had charge of the keys. N Shelley, Sec Climo at Church Square drowned 2 policemen. Case of accidental tonight, all round.*

The congregation midway through evensong in 1906 were astonished when fire brigade bugler, Gordon Jane, dashed into St Petroc's Church and sounded the alarm to summon firemen to a serious fire at Luke's Restaurant.

Around 1900, all records were broken when the horse drawn appliance raced to an intense fire at Camelford, a distance of 14 miles, in a surprising time of eighty minutes. Today I am advised that a realistic time for a modern engine would be less than thirty minutes.

17th November 1927 saw one of the most serious outbreaks of fire in Bodmin for many years, despite the efforts of four brigades. Foster Hall at the Cornwall Mental Hospital (St Lawrence) was totally destroyed. At about 8.30pm the night watchman, going on his round, discovered a small portion of the roof to be on fire and he immediately gave the alarm. Members of the hospital brigade were quickly on the scene, followed by Bodmin, Wadebridge and St Austell brigades, who had been summoned as the fire spread with alarming rapidity. The work of the firemen was seriously hampered by the fact there was a poor supply of water to cope with the flames that quickly engulfed the roof and turned the interior into a raging furnace. At one period the flames were so fierce that they lit up the countryside around and within two hours, only the four walls of what was once the finest hall of its kind in the county remained. In the interior of the building a great deal of pitch pine had been used and the flames licked this up as well as the highly polished floor. Sadly, two fine grand pianos were also destroyed. For the firemen it was a night of sheer frustration. With a good supply and pressure of water to the hydrants, the brigades would have been able to save a large portion of Foster Hall. The Bodmin brigade's motor pump was always ahead of the water supply. The hospital's manual pump was operated by nurses taking turns at the handles and the St Austell brigade was unable to use their motor engine owing to the scarcity of the water. The engine was taken down to St Lawrence's stream to pump water up to the Wadebridge steamer stationed half way between the river and the hospital. Although every effort was made the brigades were unsuccessful.

However, they did admirably succeed in stopping the flames from reaching the adjoining premises and at no time were the 1,200 patients, away in the main dormitories, at risk. In this, perhaps, they were fortunate that the wind was blowing from a south easterly direction, otherwise the sparks, volumes of which were thrown into the air in a brilliant pyrotechnic display, might have involved some of the main wards.

To the large number of townspeople who gathered and could only stand by as helpless spectators, the conflagration against the night sky presented a spectacle of awesome magnificence.

During all this, an attempt was made to turn the town water supply into the hospital pipes, but the latter were either not big enough to carry it or the special stop cocks were not opened. The town supply was, as a consequence, dammed right back to St Breward.

Until the opening of City Hall at Truro, a year or two before, Foster

Hall was the largest and best appointed in the county and was used for many important county social functions. It was erected in 1902 when the hospital was extended at the cost of £120,000 by the County Council.

The decorations in the interior were on a lavish scale and the magnificent proscenium of terracotta between the main hall and the stage, which although not destroyed, was badly discoloured, was a feature of the hall. The destruction of the hall caused great inconvenience as it was here the male patients took their meals and weekly entertainment was given; that evening a concert party from Bodmin had appeared.

Incidentally, at Wadebridge and Padstow, the firing of two rockets was the customary means of summoning the fire brigade and lifeboat men in the respective places. The firing of the rockets at Wadebridge on that Thursday evening to summon the brigade was, owing to the strong south easterly wind, also heard in Padstow, where the lifeboat men turned out, thinking they were being summoned to a ship wreck.

Foster Hall was rebuilt. Today, its future hangs in the balance, but whatever happens, it will always hold fond memories for Bodmin people who have attended shows, dances and other functions, over the years.

Foster Hall after the Fire

Toll Gates and Travel

WHEN we leave Cornwall and drive across the River Tamar Bridge to enter Plymouth we are charged a toll fee; a surcharge on our journey. I am sure most people have an opinion as to the rights or the perceived wrongs of such an imposition as they pass a payment to the toll booth.

On reading Charles Dickens – 'Pickwick Papers' we find Mr Pickwick being offered an opinion by Mr Samuel Weller senior, on the matter of turnpike keepers, as their coach bowled along the turnpike. "Werry queer life is a pike-keeper's, sir." "A what?" said Mr Pickwick. "A pike-keeper". "What do you mean by a pike-keeper?" "The old'un means a turnpike keeper, gen'lm'n", observed Mr Samuel Weller in explanation. "Oh!" said Mr Pickwick, "I see. Yes, a very curious life, very uncomfortable". "They're all on 'men as has met vith some disappointment in life" said Mr Weller senior. "Ay, ay?" said Mr Pickwick. "Yes, consequences of vich, they retires from the world and shuts themselves up in pikes; partly vith the view of being solitary and partly to rewenge themselves on mankind, by takin' tolls." "Dear me" said Mr Pickwick "I never knew that before". "Fact sir" said Mr Weller "if they was gen'lm'n you'd call 'em misanthropes but as it is, they only takes to pike-keepin".

I am not sure if the Tamar Bridge toll booth operator today would still incur the wrath of Mr Weller senior, but the choice of occupation follows a long history of charging a toll to travel on certain highways. For today's toll booth operator is yesterday's turnpike keeper.

Tollgates came into use because parish authorities, whose task it was to maintain the roads, often adopted an indifferent attitude to the problems arising from the increasing use of wheeled traffic. What were once mere tracks made by horses and pedestrians were being subjected to the passage of carts and coaches, with the result that deep ruts were formed on either side.

Parliament tried to set things right by restricting the size and weight of vehicles, passing numerous Acts designed, not so much to adapt roads to traffic as traffic to roads. There was general confusion and private enterprise stepped in. Groups of local gentry, motivated, perhaps, by a sense of social duty, as well as hope of gain, took over control of some stretches of road, towards the upkeep of which, they were allowed by the State, to erect tollgates and charge fees.

Over two centuries ago, in 1769, Bodmin's first Turnpike Act was obtained for 'widening and repairing several roads leading to and through the borough and a body of trustees was appointed for twenty one years. Their first task was to carry out the construction of the Bodmin-Launceston turnpike, which was to become the chief highway A30 through the county. No longer would there be any justification for the once popular saying 'out of the world and into Bodmin'.

Survey of 1811 – little else seems to be known of the activities of this trust until the early years of the next century. A survey of 1811 shows that it then controlled the following lengths of road: towards Truro – 11 miles; towards Wadebridge – 6 and a half miles; towards Helland – one and a half miles; towards Liskeard (via Respryn) – five and a half miles; towards Launceston – 17 and a half miles and towards St Austell (via Sweetshouse) 5 and a quarter miles.

The 'Bodmin Register' for 1831 states that fifty miles of road were under the auspices of the Bodmin Trust; an indication that the last twenty years had been spent chiefly in maintaining existing roads. The tolls then amounted to £1,451, although there was still a debt of £5,220.

The 1830s saw many new roads in the making. In 1834 a new line of improvement was ready at Lanivet, from Lamorrick Corner to Mount Pleasant via St Benet's, bypassing the old Coach Road over West Downs. According to a contemporary account *'this sequestered spot (St Benet's, Lanivet) scarcely visible in any direction at the distance of half a mile, enclosed in a deep vale and surrounded by trees, more lofty than its half-ruined tower, is by the progress of recent improvement laid open to public view and above all to the inspection of strangers. A hill so steep as to be dangerous for carriages, has to be avoided by conducting the London road through this valley.'* The same year saw the construction of the stretch of road from Bodmin to Callywith by way of Barn Park, avoiding Castle Hill.

In 1836 the road (A391) from Reperry Fork towards St Austell by way of Lockengate and Bugle was cut, but no mention of this line is made in the account book of the Bodmin Trust. An important development of the period was the completion of the present road (A38) towards Liskeard through the Glynn Valley as far as Dobwalls, for the Bodmin-Liskeard road had hitherto lain through Respryn and the Taphouses. Towards the cost of this enterprise the Liskeard Trustees gave £300 on condition that no gate was erected east of Drawbridge (near Halfway Inn) and the only one on this line of which we have record.

With the 1840s came the practice of letting the gates, the tolls being put up for auction. The collector, or turnpike keeper, was, henceforth, employed by a lessee and not by the Trust. Amusing tales are told of some of these keepers, a few of whom were seemingly not above making a little extra money for themselves. It has been said of one such fellow in the Bodmin district that he kept a jug on his table and played quoits with the sixpences received; those falling into the jug remained there for the contractor, but any falling outside he considered to be his own.

The big gate for carrier traffic was kept locked at night and after about 10 o'clock a driver wishing to pass through had to rouse the keeper. Describing the start of a journey towards Jamaica Inn in 1853 John Burton records *'the morning was dark and when we came to Callywith turnpike gate, it was closed. We knocked up Henry Mark, the old toll keeper, who looked out of the window and at first refused to let us pass till daylight. We told him that if he did not open the gate and take the 6d tolls we would unhang the gate and pass through without paying. This fetched the old chap down with his long coat, knitted white nightcap and with a horn lantern in his hand. He opened the gate and told us "you Burtons ought to be poisoned for breaking a man's rest".'* No doubt the young Burtons were amused by the fellow's incivility but in point of fact, a keeper could be fined for using offensive language to a customer; on the other hand he was similarly protected from their abuse.

St. Benet's Abbey (1842)

A millennium of Affluence - Influence - Benevolence

WHY should Bodmin be proud of its history? What makes it out as special in the annals of Cornwall? For the answer we look back to the 6th century, from when it must surely have emanated with the arrival of St Petroc, one of the most powerful of all the saints from Ireland. Following St Guron, a fellow Welshman, he founded a Christian settlement in what would have been a pagan society, his influence spreading far beyond Bodmin and Cornwall and giving the strength and purpose to make the town such a powerful place for more than a thousand years.

It was the medieval period when Bodmin, the most populous town in Cornwall, could display its power and wealth. A pilgrim visitor would have been filled with awe and wonderment at the 13 or more chapels, hospice, guild houses and a Franciscan Friary, with its church roof over 60ft high and likened by traveller historians of that period as second only to Westminster Hall. It survived until 1837 when it was partly pulled down for the building of the Assize Courts, the remains of which fell victim to making way for the Public Rooms to be erected in 1891.

The Augustinian Priory would have been a fine building. Worked stone placed near Priory Park lawn by Bodmin Old Cornwall Society give credence to the opinion that the finest masons, artisans and materials were used to make a statement of power and influence. The Priory had vast tracts of land from Portreath to Tintagel stretching inland to Lanhydrock. This was a town of considerable wealth and many families fared well under the religious dominance of the Priory. It was an administrative centre, a seat of tradecraft and considerable riches, also very much a festive place and throughout the year various denominations and guilds, all celebrated their own particular feast days with processions, pomp and merriment.

Then, during the Tudor period, that way of life for a town whose days were continually interrupted by the sounds of bells of the holy institutions, were to be witness to a revolutionary change that would dismiss a thousand years of influence, affluence and benevolence.

Always appearing to have severe matrimonial problems, it was King Henry VIII who fell out with Rome and set out to confiscate all the power and wealth accumulated by the catholic ministry, establishing the Church of England.

By 1539 Bodmin Friary and Priory had been dissolved, being sold to speculators. Chantry and guild chapels were ordered to close. It was the end of a Christian era that affected Bodmin more than any other town in Cornwall.

Today, very little is evident to the visitor. Worked stone can be found incorporated into various buildings that give an indication of a former past. It is a tragedy that no ruins remain today of a great Priory and Friary, to give a lasting remembrance of a magnificent millennium in the history of Cornwall.

A glimpse into the past can be found at Berry Tower, Cross Lane (1501-1511 AD), St Petroc's Church re-built 1469-1472, the Chantry of St Thomas Beckett immediately east of St Petroc's Church 1377 AD and exposed remains of St Petroc and Mary Church adjoining Priory House 1120 AD.

Engraved by F. Wesley, from a Drawing by F.K.L. Stockdale, for the excursions through Cornwall.
B O D M I N .

It was a Question of Hot Heads and Sore Heads really

AT the early part of the 19th century many churches in Cornwall were in a serious state of neglect and Bodmin church - St Petroc's - was no exception, as the following two items taken from newspapers in 1815 and 1816 show:

1815 - The application to Parliament, for a bill to enclose the commons around Bodmin in order to defray the expense of repairs to the church, having proved unsuccessful, the further prosecution is that very necessary undertaking has been suspended. A great part of the roof of the building is off and part of the wall is down; so that this venerable fabric is likely to become a heap of ruins; neither the Corporation, their noble patron, nor the parishioners will be at the expense of providing a place of worship for the town. At the last visitation the new church wardens refused to be sworn lest they should become liable to be prosecuted for not repairing the church.

1816 - The church at Bodmin has long been in a ruinous state and public worships have been performed in the Assize Hall; nor is there any probability that the case will be speedily altered. The Corporation are, by prescription, liable to keep the church in repair, but their funds, we understand, are inadequate to the expense which these repairs would now require. We are informed that, short time since, a meeting of the inhabitants of the borough and parish was called by the mayor, where the town clerk informed them, that the Corporation was no longer able to repair the church as their funds were wholly exhausted. They had borrowed £1,500 which was expended and their credit was so low that they could borrow no more. The inhabitants must therefore take repairs into their own hands. One of the persons present said that before the inhabitants took the repairs upon them, the Corporation should show the books that it might be clearly ascertained they were insolvent. On this the mayor addressed the person who made the observation in the following terms "You damned scoundrel; you shall never see the books".

After calling the vicar of Bodmin a liar and threatening to knock the head off the shoulders of another reverend gentleman, who was present, His Worship left the meeting which broke up in some confusion.

In the same year the Lanivet Annual Revel appeared to pick up the theme of pugilistic combat as reported by an enthusiastic onlooker.

On Sunday last, the commencement of the annual revel at Lanivet drew to the parish church-town a number of the inhabitants of Bodmin.

As soon as the service at the church was concluded the younger part of the congregation adjourned to the public house to qualify themselves for commencing their amusements with proper spirit. Here, it seems, the lads of Roche and Luxulyan showed some jealousy of the youths of Bodmin, whom they regarded as intruders. From jeers the parties proceeded to blows; but after a short skirmish the Bodmin men were overpowered by numbers and forced to make a precipitate retreat.

The sports on Monday passed without any serious disturbance; but on Tuesday the attraction of wrestling brought out a number of young persons from Bodmin; one of whom entered the ring and threw two Roche men. This success was immediately followed by an attack on the Bodmin men and a general battle commenced.

After having for some time contended in the pugilistic style, the combatants armed themselves with bludgeons from a large wood-rick in the church-town. Thus equipped, the fight was renewed with fury; heads were laid open, teeth knocked out and the field of battle was quickly strewn with the maimed. The contest continued for about two hours and victory still hung doubtful. However, by twilight the Roche and Luxulyan men were reinforced by a considerable detachment from the neighbouring mines. This fresh body of forces soon decided the fate of the day and the Bodmin men were forced to fly in disorder.

It is interesting to note that even today, parishioners have the potential to be liable to pay towards chancel repair as this recent letter from a solicitor to a house purchaser in Bodmin shows.

"A Chancel Check search has been undertaken which reveals that the property is within the historical boundary of a Parish which continues to have potential chancel repair liability.

Chancel repair liability is an ancient interest benefiting some 5,200 pre-Reformation churches in England and Wales. It allows the Parochial Church Council to require owners of former rectorial land to meet the costs of repairing the church chancel. Because the chancel of a church was the area where the rector, or parish priest, officiated, the duty of repairing the chancel of an ancient church fell on the owner of property attached to the rectory. Such rectorial land was and is not necessarily situated in close proximity to a church building. There is no single central register which can be used to identify all chancel repairs or other liabilities or restrictions attached to land and property in England and Wales, but as the obligation effects land, a new or older property can be effected."

Full Steam Ahead - The Bodmin Branch - Cutting of the First Sod

THE first sod of the proposed and long talked of branch railway from Bodmin Road station to Bodmin town was cut on Friday 23rd April 1884 and the inhabitants were in high glee at the prospect of Bodmin being at last linked to the great railway chain of the country.

Bodmin people were at one time averse to this connection, but they began to realise the great disadvantages under which they laboured consequently on being three miles from the railway, and several attempts had been made to supply the want.

When the Cornwall Railway was opened in 1859 it was proposed to approach the town by means of a central railway, but there were protests and petitions against it. They soon learnt the error of their ways however, and in 1861 they made a strong effort to get a railway by a route around Lanhydrock, the mansion and grounds of Lord Robartes.

This scheme was objected to by Lord Vivian of Glyn House and the London and South Western Rail Company. Lord Vivian petitioned against the parliamentary bill and although the London and South Western Railway Company withdrew their opposition, the expense which this opposition involved on the promoters of the scheme caused them to abandon it, after spending about £4,000; a great deal of money at that time.

The next attempt was made in 1874 when powers were sought by the Cornwall and West Cornwall Railway Companies to construct a branch from Bodmin Road station to Bodmin, terminating in a garden to the rear of the East Cornwall Bank, then in the course of erection, but this scheme proved abortive. The East Cornwall Bank today is Barclays Bank at the entrance to Priory car park.

About seven years afterwards the South Western Railway attempted to bring the railway to Bodmin by means of an extension of its line from Launceston through North Cornwall, and whilst these plans were being matured, it was ascertained that the Great Western Railway were inclined to favourably entertain a proposal to make a branch from Bodmin Road to the town if such a proposal were made.

This proposal was soon forthcoming; the Corporation offered to give the whole of the land through which the line was expected to pass and Lord Robartes afforded every facility for the furtherance of the scheme and offered to give whatever of his land that might be required.

The Great Western soon promoted a bill, encouraged no doubt by this liberality, somewhat unusual in connection with railway extensions. It was, of course, opposed by Lord Vivian, but his objections proved futile and the bill was passed. In due course a contract was arranged with Mr Griffith Griffiths and it was hoped the pick and shovels of a full detachment of navvies would soon be busily at work on the route. The line would terminate in Bodmin, in a field a little beyond St Nicholas Street and near the new barracks. The work was estimated to cost from £40,000 to £50,000 and was expected to be completed in about eighteen months.

The day of the ceremony was observed in the town as a general holiday and hundreds poured in from surrounding districts to participate in the day's enjoyment. The decorations extended as far as Bodmin Road station where the road was spanned by an evergreen arch, surmounted with a wheel barrow laden with turf and a pick and shovel. Several arches of similar construction were erected in various parts of the town and bore mottos appropriate to the occasion, such as 'Success to the Bodmin Railway', 'Progress' and so on. Beautiful trees were temporarily planted in the principal streets and there was a profuse display of flags obtained from the Devonport Dockyard through the kind intervention of the Hon E F Leveson-Gower, the member for the borough at Westminster.

The directors of the Great Western Railway travelled by special train from Plymouth to Bodmin Road station and arrived in Bodmin shortly after 2 o'clock. Lord Lyttleton, speaking on behalf of the railway company presented the mayor, Mr T Baron, with a beautiful silver engraved spade with a polished pine handle for cutting the first sod.

In 1887, in pursuance of a resolution recently passed by public meeting, the inhabitants of Bodmin on a Friday evening provided supper in the Market House for the men who had been engaged in constructing the new branch railway and to commemorate the close of their labours. The 170 men who had been involved marched from Mount Folly headed by the band of the 3rd Battalion DCLI and the Bodmin Fife and Drum band. After the supper the mayor thanked the men and told them that the entertainment given was solely on account of the exemplary behaviour whilst engaged on the line of the railway. Four or five men, in brief and intelligent speeches expressed their gratitude to the mayor and people of Bodmin.

The branch railway is today operated by the Bodmin & Wenford railway carries around 50,000 passengers per year.

Wells, Springs and Holy Things, Rushes, Rags and Pagan Pins -Bodmin's Well Trail

BEFORE the Dissolution of the mid 1500s, Bodmin was a citadel of churches, chapels, hospitals, guild houses, a friary and a priory that owned vast lands stretching from Portreath to Tintagel on the north coast and inland as far as Lanhydrock. Today traces of this magnificent age can be found dotted around the town; survivors of all the cultural and social upheavals throughout the centuries. Among them are the holy wells that first attracted the town's original inhabitants.

Holy wells were once frequented by devotees in search of health, omens or predictions of coming events. Many of the wells were believed to possess curative properties for warts, sore and weak eyes, lameness, rheumatism and even leprosy. Some were used as wishing wells by young men and young women who threw a crooked pin into the water and wished at the same time. Love divination was practised, where pins made from points of blackthorn were thrown into the water; if they sank, the lover was not sincere. Rushes were woven into a cross and likewise thrown onto the water; if the cross sank it foretold of disaster within one year. The habit of tying rags to the branches of a tree close to the well was also practised, being done mainly by people suffering from maladies. The rag was first dipped in the water and the afflicted part of the body bathed with it. The rag was then tied to the branch of a nearby tree so the healing properties of the well could act upon it.

Some of the superstitions originate from pre-Christian times, when water was an object of worship and veneration. Offerings of cakes, pins or coins, were made either to the water itself or to the deity of the spring. This was resented by the Roman Church and in 960AD, the Saxon king, Edgar, commanded by cannon law: "That every priest industriously advance Christianity and extinguish heathenism and forbid the worship of fountains and necromancy and auguries". But, finding the worship of springs so deeply rooted, many of the wells were re-dedicated to a saint. Churches were frequently erected on the spot and a priest provided, baptising his flock in the water of the well. Nevertheless, many pagan customs of well worship lingered on from generation to generation and people still visit wells for their traditional virtues, be it for healing or for divination.

In 2001 Bodmin Town Forum initiated the Holy Wells and Springs project and with funding in place carried out major restoration work to the wells and immediate area within the parish.

St Guron's Well House

To walk the trail, start at St Petroc's Well situated at the east end of Priory Park Football Ground. A complete restoration of the area surrounding the Well was undertaken by the Environment Agency in 2001 as part of the flood alleviation scheme to the Town Leat - the stream flowing through and under the town. Today, only the top third is visible and due to its close proximity to the modern works that have taken place it will need sympathetic landscaping to preserve its integrity for future generations.

The next visit will be St Guron's Well and Well House at the top of St Petroc's Church steps. The earliest reference appears in the 12th century 'life of St Petroc's' where it is said he built two habitations, in a place where Vuron (Guron) had lived, in the valley by the Well.

Well number three is the Eye Well (Bree Shute Well) situated near the car park off Dennison Road, which had a reputation for its healing properties and like St Guron's Well is a Grade II Listed Building. Continue on down Dennison Road to the junction with Chapel Lane, where you will find Cock's Well, dated 1849, which supplied water for local inhabitants as well as the blacksmith, whose smithy stood opposite.

Finally, Well number five, Scarlett's Well, just off the Camel Trail, named after the Scarlett family who had provided three MPs for the town between 1312 and 1341. The well was refurbished in 1995 by the Bodmin Old Cornwall Society. At one period in the Middle Ages its fame was such 'that folk ran flocking thither in huge numbers from all quarters' (Carew circa 1600).

The Holy wells and springs play an important role in Bodmin's history and in recognition, an excellent leaflet was produced for the Forum by Heulyn Lewis of North Cornwall District Council, which guides you along the trail, giving a fully descriptive explanation on the history of each Well and taking you on a walk of discovery from the east to the west of the parish. The leaflet is of high quality and can be obtained from the Bodmin Visitor Information Centre, Shire Hall, Bodmin; so why not pick one up and enjoy walking the Bodmin Well Trail. After all, it is our heritage.

Out of the Mire - A Generous Trans-Atlantic Solution

PRIORY Park, Bodmin has been the home of Bodmin Town Football Club for over fifty years; its setting surely ensures it as one of the finest grounds in the south west. The Club, founded in 1889 by Mr W M Pethybridge and Mr C H Bray, is one of the oldest clubs in Cornwall and shared its centenary year with the Cornwall County Football Association (CCFA). Bodmin originally played at Cooksland (off the Liskeard Road) then moved to Coldharbour Lane, Barn Park, back to Cooksland, then to Westheath and finally to Priory Park.

In 1956, a decision was made to complement the two laid out pitches by the erection of a large stand alongside pitch number one. It was a difficult decision. At that time the ground had been excavated to provide a flat playing surface, which was achieved, but regrettably the under-surface work, the key drainage and bed of the pitches was not satisfactory and created monumental problems. In 1958, following the previous two seasons, Mr Fred Peel-Yates, who wrote under the pseudonym of 'Fan Fare', lamented in the local newspaper, *"When the Priory Park scheme was launched and developed, the two football pitches became two quagmires in early winter and remained that way until spring weather came along to dry them out. Since the failure of the Priory pitches, the Town Council has had the courage to have them laid out properly. Something not done in the first place!"*

Across the Atlantic, in Canada, Mr T H (Harry) Dennison, who received regular postings of the local paper read the original decision and was influenced to help the sporting fraternity in his former home town. The article referred to the need of a new stand for the football field and noted the Town Council could not afford the balance of the cost.

Mr Dennison thought hard about this for fifteen months and then made an offer of £750 to enable matters to proceed. It then came as a surprise to him when the Council informed him they still could not finance the balance of the project. Subsequently he increased his offer to cover the cost of the stand. He said he would always remember with gratitude the first twenty years of his life in the town of Bodmin. He then increased the donation to £1500, as he was not prepared to have anything erected he did not regard as fully worthy of the town. The gift was further increased to £2500 (today in the region of £50,000) when he was again informed that owing to even more commitments it was still not possible for the Town Council to undertake further expense.

By kind permission of David Sandry

The new stand with seating for 450 spectators was formally opened by Mr Dennison, accompanied by his sister, Maud, on Wednesday 10th September 1958. To mark the occasion, an unveiling of a commemorative plaque above the entrance to the stand took place – *Dennison Memorial Stand - dedicated by T H Dennison Esq of Toronto, Honorary Freeman of this Borough. In memory of the Dennison family 10th September 1958.*

There then followed a game between Bodmin and Cornwall, the Cornwall side winning 8-1. After the game the players and officials were entertained to an official dinner at the Royal Hotel. During the evening Mr Dennison made a surprise presentation of wallets containing a sum of money to each of the players. In his speech he stated he was aware that the rooms under the stand had yet to be finished, but there would be a chance to complete that work, bit by bit, while games were being played on the other pitch. There was accommodation for a coffee bar, showers, changing rooms for teams and rooms for referee and linesmen. There were no pillars to obstruct the view and he thought there was no finer fireproof stand in Cornwall.

Sutton Seeds, Turf consultants to the Town Council, gave permission for that special game to be played, but the pitch would not be in regular use for over a year.

Only six days before the opening of the grandstand the Council convened a special meeting to admit as Honorary Freemen of the Borough, - HRH Prince Chula Chakrabongse of Thailand and Mr T H Dennison.

The stand, fifty years old this month, has served the town well for all the many events and matches that have taken place during these past fifty years. It is hoped that its future replacement will be equally successful.

A Living Testament to a Proud Past

FACING Church Square in Bodmin is the parish church of St Petroc which, together with the 14th century chapel of St Thomas Becket and the vicarage, represents an important complex of ecclesiastical buildings.

The church is Cornwall's largest parish church and is a Grade 1 Listed Building of national significance.

The church has a long history and is located on the probable site of St Petroc's monastery in the 9th and 10th centuries and by 1086 the Domesday Book noted 'Bodmine' by St Petroc Church had 68 houses and a market; Bodmin had clearly become a small town.

After the Norman Conquest, the town extended westwards and the monastery moved a short distance to what we know today as Priory House and grounds. At this time the old monastic church became the parochial church for priory tenants. It was rebuilt in 1469/72; however the only surviving elements from the Norman period are the base of the tower and the outstanding granite font.

To have built this church within three or four years is really quite remarkable, as in 1351, and subsequently afterwards, the Black Death or plague had decimated the population, but having said that, Bodmin throughout its history, has always shown resilience.

When rebuilt, the tower originally had a 150 feet spire – an unusual feature on a Cornish church of this period – which was added to in the time of, or by, Prior Vivian (d 1533). Thomas Tonkin recorded in December 1699 that 'the beautiful spire there, esteemed the loftiest and fairest in the west, was destroyed by lightening, by which it sunk down into the square tower under'.

The Christian relationship with the site of the church goes back to the first saints to settle there i.e. St Guron, followed by St Petroc in the 6th century. The spring that still brings a constant flow of water would have been a strong influence with the Celtic saints who chose to settle there; flowing today through St Guron's Well and out through the gargoyles at the foot of the church steps. It has never been known to run dry, proving to be a constant reliable source when at times over the years all other water was scarce and often polluted.

Early records indicate that possibly the original monastic church was built over St Guron's Well because of the sacred association of the spring. Certainly, when the church was rebuilt it did suffer badly with water incursion and by the early 1800s it was recorded that the church was full of springs and sometimes in the winter it flooded. Considerable work was carried out including the forming of a deep 'spacious trench' all around the church and as a result of these improvements 'the whole edifice has been rendered perfectly dry'.

The church was suffering badly at this time; lack of funds – a serious problem for such a large church, and falling congregation numbers. In 1815 a bill was brought before parliament to empower the mayor and burgess of Bodmin (who had found themselves responsible) to enclose and sell common land for the purpose of repairing the church and providing a new market house. This proved to be highly unpopular with the town's people to such a degree that there was considerable rioting and disturbance. The militia was called in and that portion of the bill removed. It is not always wise to ignore or not consult public opinion.

It is a wonderful building which sits proudly within Cornwall's rich heritage of ecclesiastical architecture and well worth visiting.

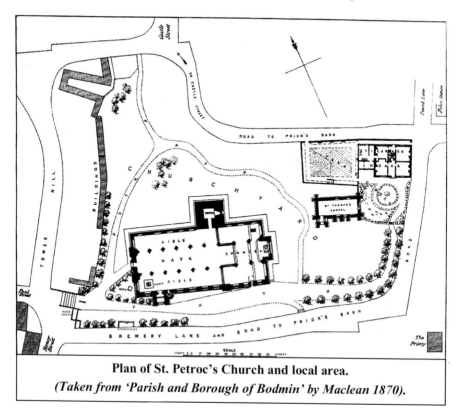

Plan of St. Petroc's Church and local area.
(Taken from 'Parish and Borough of Bodmin' by Maclean 1870).

I see no Castles! When is a Castle not a Castle?

IF the question was posed as to which would be the earliest part of any established settlement, the answer would, in all probability, point to the church. Religion, in one form or another has always been central to a community; the pillar that gave strength and direction. That was the required thinking throughout centuries and settlements were built on that premise and to a degree, worked.

However, a puzzle still remains in Bodmin as to whether there were two religious settlements; one around the site of St Petroc's Church and another to the north in the area we know as Berry Tower. To be able to reach Berry Tower from the church you would take the ancient highway known as Castle Street, but where, you may ask, was the castle? Bodmin lacks the magnificence and splendour of a castle in its midst, as for example Launceston has; in fact it lacks any real castle or remains.

The name 'Castle' could easily pre-date the solid built castles we associate with the medieval period; we may have to go back to the Iron Age period. Think, for example of Castle Canyke, to the east of the town, the largest Iron Age fort in Cornwall. In the parishes around Bodmin there are sites of defended farmsteads or rounds; the names 'Berry' and 'Castle' may record the presence of another enclosed site of that period.

A suggestion has been put forward that Bodmin was the site of a monastery named Dinuurrin around 800AD and may have been built on a hill to the north of the centre of Bodmin. There are a number of place names which include the element 'berry' in the immediate area with documentary evidence. The word derives from the Old English *burb* meaning a defended site and therefore suggests a link with the Cornish element *din*, a fort, which occurs in Dinuurrin. Looking at the physical topography it would give a possible location to the east of Castle Hill House, on the upper part of Castle Hill. Castle Street was first recorded in 1313 as 'Castel' Street.

In 1994 North Cornwall District Council designated the old cemetery and land surrounding Berry Tower, Cross Lane, Bodmin, a total of 10 acres, a Conservation Area. The main effects or key elements of such a designation are:

The Planning Authority advertises all planning applications that are likely to affect the character and appearance of the area;

With certain minor exceptions no building or part of a building can be demolished or removed without consent;

No tree can be lopped or felled without consent;

The Council examines applications for planning permission and advertisement consent very carefully to ensure any new development accords with the architectural and visual qualities of the area.

Ten years later a restoration project was completed to the early 16th century Berry Tower.

On Saturday 15th November 2008 at 2.15pm, we opened Berry Tower to enable people to visit and climb up the internal staircase and ladders to the top of the tower. This was followed by a walk around the old cemetery to look at various headstones of interest. Mr Nick Prideaux, Bodmin Town Cryer complete with his bell, delivered a 'cry' of welcome to one and all from the top of the 50ft tower, a most impressive performance not lost upon those who were there to witness it. We shared the afternoon with Cornwall Wildlife Trust who were recording various fungi to be found, together with the Cornwall Fungi Recording Group who were looking for lichens proving what a valuable asset Berry Tower cemetery is with its history and its nature conservation. It is a conservation area that we should all cherish for what it is.

A Fragment of Medieval Bodmin - Huge Granite Fireplace -a Reminder of Wealthy and Powerful Times

TODAY, 24 Fore Street, Bodmin trades as The Edinburgh Woollen Mills presenting an attractive frontage, concealing its true history within. It was probably built in the 1600s as a merchant's house, with its frontage re-modelled in the 1700s along with other premises in the bottom end of Fore Street. Today, it is a Listed Building in a Conservation Area and recent changes to the shop front have been made maintaining a sympathetic approach, without loss of character, which sits well within the overall main street scene.

Thanks to the previous owners, Mr and Mrs Shelley, the most important feature was protected during their trading years and today Edinburgh Woollen Mills reveals the massive granite fireplace as a feature at the far end of the store. For years it was known that a huge fireplace was situated within the building, but which few people had seen. In 1968 Mr and Mrs Shelley brought it to the attention of the curator at the County Museum, Mr H L Douch, who, on seeing it for the first time, when it was only half uncovered, black with soot and grime, so much so it was not easy to determine the stone it was made from, was of the opinion that it was not very prepossessing. The fact that the shop is adjacent to the old Guildhall building (now Malcolm Barnecutt's Restaurant and offices) gave rise to the view, among those who study the history of Bodmin, that the fireplace could well have been part of the original Guildhall, which was initially a meeting place for the town's various craft and trade guilds, numbering about 40. No doubt it was also the borough's civic centre.

Mr Douch inspected the fireplace, with its strongly carved massive lintel, which at some time had been vertically fractured down the middle and joined again. The carved stone fireplace had long been known to older Bodmin people, but few outside the town and indeed many residents, would not have been aware of its existence. Only the fireplace itself and the great depth of the chimney wall give any indication that the premises were once important. The other walls are insubstantial and the building as ordinary as one might find behind shops in a Cornish street.

Originally, however, this finely carved moor stone lintel and supporting piers must have formed the main architectural feature of a large hall. One wonders what type of establishment it served. The Priory buildings were some distance away; the Friary was nearer, but this did not appear to be part of it.

Now the fireplace stands suggestively near a more modern former Guildhall, virtually in the centre of the town. Such a hearth would have fitted the dignity of the mayor and corporation beginning to assert their claims against the increasingly autocratic Prior. The style of its decoration is reminiscent of wood carving in the late 15th and early 16th centuries. One might therefore suggest that the chief burgesses celebrated here when the monasteries were finally dissolved and they escaped from the control of the Priors. In a later century the hall became dilapidated and shrank in subsequent re-building. The fireplace and chimney stack were retained, perhaps from sentiment, but more likely because of their massive strength. This part of the hall was converted to everyday uses. The old floor, paved with spar stones, each about the size of a fist, was raised to give easier access to the steeply rising ground at the back. At different times the huge chimney space was adapted and contracted to suit plainer needs. First the back wall was built up, and into this increased depth was put a cloam oven; its aperture and part of its beehive roof are still in position. Later, a free standing wall cut the depth of the space even more, an iron stove was put flush with the front of the hearth and the unused half of the chimney space walled up.

By this time the massive stone lintel had cracked and the additional safeguard of an oak beam was inserted above it in order to take some of the weight of the chimney. A further alteration was the insertion of a second cloam oven at the side of the old fireplace. This was a small oven and in the top right hand corner there was impressed the name of the maker – G Fishley, Fremington. (George Fishley was a cloam oven maker and potter at Fremington, North Devon, in the late 18th and 19th century). Barnstaple, Bideford and Fremington had a number of potteries due to the availability of the right kind of clay needed.

In the rubble which was used to raise the floor level there were pieces of pillar and tracery worked stone which had evidently been brought from the ruined ecclesiastical buildings nearby; one can expect to find these on most sites near the centre of Bodmin. There were also broken crocks, medicine bottles, a trivet, cast iron pots and the usual household bric-a-brac of the late 18th and 19th centuries.

More unusual were a two handled mortar used for grinding down powders and three items that recall the Belling family of clockmakers from nearby. One was an ivory pocket sundial and others, brass date and hour rings from clock faces.

When the Edinburgh Woollen Mills carried out refurbishment, they found there were three floors on the first floor, as each floor had worn out; another was placed on top of it.

Bodmin has always played a pivotal role in Cornwall's affairs and throughout the medieval period it was a turbulent time, when the town was either wealthy or experiencing extreme poverty, rebellions and civil war and was faced with an uneasy future.

The ancient hall may have long gone, but the fireplace, its granite taken off the moor and carved and shaped 600 years ago, has born witness to the journey through the history of both Bodmin and Cornwall.

Excavation of the Old Fireplace in Shelley's shop, Fore Street.
Note the two cloam ovens – one within the fireplace and the other at the side.

The White Hart with a Royal Connection

THE Bodmin Register recorded for May 1831, twenty nine public and beer houses within the borough, so one could confidently assume with a population of around 4,000 that the town was well served.

Of the old inns only a few trade today. One is the 'White Hart' originally situated near the library, Lower Bore Street, and that site itself was the Western Inn whose landlord was known as 'Seven-Belly Williams'. It was said he was a person of stout proportions. The Sherborne Mercury of September 1754 reported – we are assured from Cornwall that Mr Lewis, master of *The White Hart* at Bodmin has, at his own expense erected milestones for 22 miles over the large moors that lay between Launceston and Bodmin: the road that was difficult before that, those not acquainted with it used to choose to take a circuit of 33 miles to pass from one town to the other, though the way over the moors is no more than 24 miles. In 1787 it was one of the stops for the Royal Mail. The mail coaches ran to and from Exeter and Falmouth in 16 hours, three times a week, with a guard provided by the government. However, within twenty years its posting business had gone and by the 1850s the sign appeared in Pool Street on the inn formerly known as the *Golden Lion.*

The obituary of Mrs Thomas May 1941 mentioned the following: Walter Verran became licensee in succession to his father and grandfather, his sister, Mrs Thomas, succeeded him and now her daughter (Mrs Watson) holds the licence. Thus, the fourth generation of one family to become licensee, a record of continuity believed to be unique in Cornwall. Until the year 1918 the *White Hart* brewed its beer on the premises, the last in the borough to do so. A Mr J Welch was solely responsible for brewing the beer, in those days two pence a pint.

There is a connection with the *White Hart* in Launceston, for in 1767 the front of the house was rebuilt of Launceston red brick (from Leworthy, Lawitton) and the interior refurbished. The new long room was described as the largest in the county. In 1774, Mr Thomas Prockter of *'The Swan'* Exeter, moved in. In January 1776 he declared "it is greatly improved" and described it as "having three dining rooms and three parlours and be able to make up sixty beds and stable sixty horses and with three neat post-chaises with twelve able horses". Widow of Thomas, Mrs Prockter became landlady. Widowed for five years she married Robert Pape of *'The Cremyll Passage Inn'*, part owner of *'The White Hart'* in Bodmin.

Although the *White Hart* at Launceston was a coaching inn, it was the arrival of the mail coach one evening that caused great consternation to all those present. A new bridge was erected in 1835 at Polson to cross the River Tamar, during the erection of which a curious coach mishap took place. The London mail coach, due at Launceston at a quarter past eleven at night, drew up one evening as usual at the *Arundel Arms*, Lifton and the driver, passengers and guard dismounted, Mr Wilson, agent of the Duke of Northumberland being the only person left in the vehicle.

The horses, which included a blind near-leader, suddenly bolted and galloped towards Launceston, and having crossed the temporary wooden bridge at the foot of the very steep hill, without accident, eventually halted driverless and breathless at the *White Hart*, Launceston, their accustomed stopping place.

They were followed by the guard, Cornelius Crowhurst, who had thrown himself on horseback immediately he had discovered their flight and was delighted to find all was well.

The *White Hart* is a popular inn sign within Cornwall and a possible explanation could be that Edward the Black Prince, the first Duke of Cornwall, who resided from time to time at Restormel Castle, married his cousin Joan, whose surviving son, afterwards Richard II, obtained the distinguishing badge of the white hart (or hind) from his mother, which was worn by his courtiers. Another possible origin is this account by Sir Halliday Wagstaffe, Keeper of the Woods and Forests in the reign of King Henry VII. The King fancied a day's hunting and rode to the New Forest for that purpose. A celebrated white hart, called Albert, a noble looking animal, was selected for the day's sport. Albert showed them some fine running and the chase continued till nearly close of day, when, after being hard pressed by the dogs, he crossed a river near Ringwood and finally stood at bay in a meadow. His pursuers came up just at the time the dogs were about to make a sacrifice of their victim, when the ladies interceded for the noble animal. Their intercession was listened to and the dogs called off and the animal secured. Albert was led into Ringwood where a gold collar was placed around his neck before he was taken to Windsor. That day Halliday Wagstaffe was knighted in Ringwood. The house of entertainment at which the King and his courtiers partook of some refreshment had its sign altered to that of the White Hart.

During the mid nineteenth century, despite low wages, there was much drunkenness. Gin drinking became so common that the Government allowed beer shops to open at pleasure. To combat liquor being sold without duty, the Government passed an Act allowing licensees to sell spirits etc at a fee of two guineas and such premises were known as 'Kiddlewinks'. The result was that thousands of these sprang up in a very short time and these and pubs were found in every village and town.

Bodmin had many public houses and inns, whose hours of business were from 6am to midnight. These included the *London Inn* at the top of Honey Street, the *Fountain Inn* on Mount Folly, the *George and Dragon* in St Nicholas Street, the *Cornish Arms* in Crockwell Street, the *White Hart* in Pool Street, the *Queen's Head, Royal Hotel* and *Town Arms* in Fore Street; the *Barley Sheaf, Mason's Arms, Garland Ox* and the *New Inn* in Bore Street and Higher Bore Street, as well as the *Railway Inn*, the *Globe Inn* and the *Board* (off licence).

Cornishman, Sir Arthur Quiller-Couch reminisced that when the steam engine was invented, away went the stage coaches. The roads were comparatively deserted; inns put up their shutters and their stable roofs tumbled in. Years passed and the internal combustion engine was invented; the traffic flowed back along the highways, inns opened again and became hotels and the stables were turned into garages.

Thanks to Mr Jim Edwards, local historian, Launceston, for information included in this article.

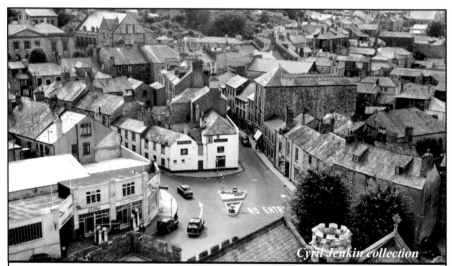

Church Square, Bodmin. In the centre of the photograph is the *'Duke of Cornwall'* pub formerly the *'Globe Inn'*. (Date: ca.1960).

Moor's Jubilee Rock - A Celebration with a Dash of Patriotic Spirit

VISIT Pendrift Downs, just north of the attractive moorland village of Blisland and you will come across a prominent feature in the landscape, Jubilee Rock. This massive granite boulder sits high above the De Lank valley with commanding views that include the River Camel estuary.

It is now nearly two centuries ago that the intense loyalty to the throne by Lieutenant John Rogers, a 24-year-old army officer of the 65th regiment, inspired him to create a lasting memorial to commemorate the jubilee of King George III.

The 20ft by 14ft (6.5m x 4.25m) boulder was laboriously carved, firstly with the figure of Britannia holding out the olive branch of peace to the world and by her side the Cornish coat of arms surmounted by its plume of feathers and famed motto 'One and All'.

Other carvings include the royal coat of arms, the arms of local prominent families including the Molesworths, Morsheads, Boscawen and Rogers. The Boscawen and Molesworth families were joint owners of Pendrift at that time. The Rogers family dated back to the days of William the Conqueror, when two brothers named Rogers settled in this country. One branch settled at Blisland and the other at St Breward.

Further carvings have the Masonic insignia and symbols of Industry, Agriculture, Plenty and Commerce, a square and compass carved at two corners of the almost flat top of the boulder and at the end of 19th century someone else inscribed 'V R 1897' - Queen Victoria's diamond jubilee year.

Lieutenant Rogers hoped his efforts would inspire recruitment to the regiment and dined with his recruiting party on Jubilee Rock on 25th October 1810; but after all his efforts it is sad to say the Rogers family coat of arms was obliterated by some person unknown.

The lettering has, from time to time been painted but due to the exposed nature of the site and being lashed by moorland rain, some of the carvings are difficult to trace and need to be read when the sun is at the right angle. As we approach the year 2010, two hundred years after John Roger's efforts, it would, perhaps, make a very worthwhile project for restoration in a parish famed for its skill in working granite.

Jubilee Rock - Pendrift Downs, Bodmin Moor, Blisland Parish.

I am delighted to report that in 2010 Blisland Parish Council carried out excellent restoration work and on a bright sunny October Sunday afternoon a celebration was held at Jubilee Rock to mark the 200 years. The Parish should be proud of their efforts that will enable future generations to pause and appreciate the elaborate carvings in the same way as their forefathers.

History and Mystery on Bodmin Moor

ROUGH Tor, in the mid 1800s, became a focal point for the Temperance Societies to hold meetings at which the perils of alcohol were preached and encouragement given to sign the pledge and lead a life of propriety. They were very popular, with as many as three thousand people attending. The local publicans took note of what was happening and sensed a business opportunity; so whilst the Temperance were at the top of Rough Tor preaching hell fire and damnation to those who took to the evils of drink, down below, the publicans set up booths to serve the thousand or so people who attended and who were perhaps less committed than the brethren gathered on high. The Temperance Society did win the day eventually and the booths ceased, and with it the drunken and riotous behaviour that inevitably took place over a long day.

A 'great revel' had been advertised in the previous century, to take place at Dozmary Pool, Midsummer day, 1773 and the local paper of the day, the Sherborne Mercury, reported a 'good boat' having been procured for gentlemen and ladies to take to the water, but mentioned those who refused to pay the penny per horse admission would be charged with trespass.

Dozmary Pool is reputedly bottomless, but a farmer in the 1800s opened a ditch close by which caused the pool to dry out; the average depth, when full would be around four feet!

If you believe in legend, Sir Bedivere threw the enchanted sword, Excalibur, into the depth of the pool after King Arthur was slain.

Another most famous legend concerns the wicked steward at Lord Robartes family home, Lanhydrock. Tregeagle was the worst of the worst and in death was forced to atone for his sins. He was tasked to empty Dozmary Pool with a limpet shell with a hole in the centre for good measure. Though, of course, he did have a respite when the farmer emptied the pool.

The period of the 1880s/90s saw a commercial use for the pool. The weather was much more extreme than we experience today and the fishing industry in Looe needed ice to pack around the fish to preserve them in transit to London. The Dozmary Pool Ice Works came into being to supply the need. Ice harvested from the pool was stored in a stone-lined platform cut into the hillside on its north bank, then covered by slabs of peat for insulation. When offered for sale, the business had developed considerably. that is, a large well constructed timber-lined store capable of holding 500 or 600 tons of ice, a substantial house in which the Overseer of the works resided, a new engine house containing a new engine and boiler, hydraulic press, every appliance for compressing ice on a large scale, a jetty and lines of a tramway with turntables.

Looking back it could be seen that they were making ice using a machine fuelled by peat that was capable of turning an area of the pool into thick ice, which could then be split into large blocks. These blocks of ice were then hauled up a ramp and stored in the ice house. Horse and wagon would transport the ice, when required, to Doublebois or Liskeard railway stations. The ice works ceased trading in 1900.

It is hard to believe that such a lonely place as Dozmary Pool could have witnessed such industrial activity as took place over a period of twenty years. But, of course, this was the Victorian Industrial era and many things were made possible.

For me, Dozmary Pool, at dusk as the mist rolls in and hearing the curlew in the marsh land is truly Bodmin Moor and a haunting memory that stays with you forever.

Butterstor looking towards Roughtor

The Ever Changing Face of Bodmin Moor

BODMIN Moor did not suffer the Ice Age but was near enough to the ice-bound areas to be subject to considerable changes of temperature. It became sodden during the summer months, frozen during the cold spells and in thaw periods the sludge crept down the hills bringing heavy boulders sliding down, resulting in heaps of rocks on the hill slopes. Roughtor is an easily accessible example with long lines of rocks moved down by sludge.

By the time of the Bronze Age period, around 2500 BC, the moor gradually settled; the climate was conducive to farming and evidence of that age can be seen every day when out walking, such as the circular bases of their houses, adjoining field hedge boundaries, ceremonial stone circles, standing stones and burial chambers; the list is long, fascinating and worthy of much exploration.

A deteriorating climate led to settlements being abandoned by 1000 BC. With the moor being used for rough summer grazing, Iron Age man was better equipped to clear woodland in the valleys than his predecessor and such areas would be more attractive to him. However, these were troubled times and the hill forts and defended settlements fringing the moor give a clear indication of how life had changed from the former pastoral scene of a previous millennium; or at least how we envisage how life had been.

By the middle of the medieval period, population growth saw resettlements taking place again; many in the form of hamlets consisting of two or more farmsteads. To be sustainable many undertook the process of tin streaming the streams and marshes. A useful indication of the age of settlements is the words in the Cornish language e.g. *Tre* (a farm or settle-ment), *Bos* (dwelling) and *Pen* (headland). Although average temperatures rose during this time, upland farming would always be difficult with the thin acid soil cover and extremes of weather patterns.

The longhouse became the farmhouse, a rectangular building built out from a hillside and housing the cattle at one end during the winter months, with a central passageway to divide the cattle from the household.

Devastation arrived during the fourteenth century in the form of the plague, Black Death. Millions died and the effects were immediate on the moor; the survivors being in demand by landowners who became desperate for farm workers; although many left for better land and more agreeable weather patterns off the moor. There were rich pickings to be bargained for, leading to the small hamlets becoming a single farm for those who chose to remain.

The nineteenth century saw an expansion again linked to population increase and industrial activities taking place around St Cleer with mining and substantial quarry undertakings, but as in previous times, when the demand dropped many of the farms collapsed and reverted to moorland. The moor immediately around Bolventor is a good example of mid-eighteenth century intake with its straight large rectangular field patterns.

Farming and living has never been easy in upland areas and no matter how many screens we watch or how rapid our source of information, we have to live with our climate and everything nature chooses to place in our path. Generations of moorland farmers have done just that.

By the early eighteen hundreds there were 23000 hectares of open, unenclosed moorland. Today this figure would relate to 9400 hectares; the main losses being attributed to nineteenth century enclosures for crops, World War Two when a great deal of land was ploughed for crops and forestry, three large reservoirs, china clay extraction, airfields and major road improvements. The pressure today on planners means that Cornwall is in danger of shrinking its environmental landscape even more. In October 1999 I wrote as a foreword for the Bodmin project "Bodmin Moor is a recognised environmental area of national status but has a need to economically sustain those who live and work there". This is still an ongoing sincere belief, with ever increasing awareness that Bodmin Moor cannot afford to lose or suffer any further major intrusions whatsoever into its existing landscape.

Garrow Farm, 17thC farmhouse in the heart of Bodmin Moor. ©PD

Watchet – There is Clay on the Way

BODMIN Moor has always a challenge to those who wish to exploit minerals, as with all upland areas the topography, climate and remoteness have been a major constraint. Frank Parkyn was a man who liked a challenge. Born in 1850 near Lerryn, son of a prosperous wool merchant, he was sent to live at Durfold in Blisland as it was considered the moorland air would be beneficial to his health.

He became aware of the clay deposits within the Blisland/Temple areas of Bodmin Moor and the rapid expansion taking place around St Austell to meet an ever-growing market. With the support of the trustees of the late James Hayward, one of the principal landowners, he was able to work land for china clay from about 1870 at Durfold and Temple.

Transportation to the railway presented a major problem and was costly, with having to transport clay by horse and wagon through the narrow lanes with rutted surfaces and high hedge banks, together with limited passing places. His answer was to lay a gravity feed line of pipes to bring the clay slurry down off the moor to clay drying sheds he had built alongside the Bodmin and Wadebridge Railway at Stump Oak, Tresarrett beneath Blisland. This represented a first for Bodmin Moor and brought a reduction in time and costs to the point of despatch but, however, there were many more hurdles to negotiate before the customer received the order.

Records show consignments to regular customers in Cheshire and Somerset: We can follow a consignment to Watchet in Somerset where there were two key players, Mr Parkyn, who wished to despatch the then dried blocks of clay and Mr Hayes Kyd, superintendent of the Bodmin and Wadebridge Railway Company at the railway headquarters in Wadebridge, who also acted as a shipping agent; a very busy man, not helped in those days when all communication was by post or telegraph.

Hayes Kyd would be advised by letter of tonnage and destination and instructed to procure a vessel for shipment. This would eventually be achieved but not without a lengthy haggle over tonnage price. The size of the vessel would dictate whether they could load direct at Wadebridge and save time or have to load barges and be taken to Padstow.

In the 1870s the whole process from booking a vessel to freight on board could take seventeen days to a month, with a great deal of hand written correspondence between all the parties. For Hayes Kyd not only had to ensure shipping but also railway wagons to bring the clay to the wharf at

Wadebridge in good time, as loading to meet tide times was crucial.

Frank Parkyn set the pattern for moving clay off the moor to dries built alongside railway lines for ease of loading and transport. Stannon Pit to Wenford Dries closed in 2000; Hawks Tor to Newbridge Sidings (Glyn Valley) closed 1971; Glyn Valley (Temple) to Bodmin Road Station closed 1942; Park (St Neot) to Moorswater, Liskeard closed 1997.

Today no china clay is quarried on Bodmin Moor. The challenges of yesteryear are no more but the industrial remains are still there to remind us of a fascinating period in our history.

My thanks to Keith Searle for allowing me to quote from documents in his possession.

Abb. 1 **Bodmin** (5500 Einw.), zwischen **Bodmin Moor** (b) (419 m) im NO und **Hensbarrow** (313 m) im SW gelegen, c der von Wäldern begleitete River Camel. Oben rechts der SW-Rand des von Heiden und Mooren bedeckten Bodmin Moors (b), k der südlichste der drei K a o l i n g r u b e n b e z i r k e am W-Rand von Bodmin Moor

The River Tamar - not always what it seems

THE journey through life that we all undertake could be looked upon as the journey of a river, issuing forth from mother earth to take those first few tentative steps from rivulet to stream, eager to explore and full of energy, to gradually emerge into adulthood with a sense of purpose and experience that takes one through to reach the estuary and sea, the journey complete.

One such river is the Tamar, rising in high moorland close to the north coast, its beauty invites legend, and we are not disappointed, for we have Tamara.

Legend has it that the Tamar is said to be given its name from Tamara, a beautiful nymph who lived under the earth. She was unhappy, however, with these surroundings and longed for the sunshine and flowers of the earth above. So, secretly, she would leave her home and roam about the countryside. On one of her wanderings she met two giants, Tavy and Tawridge (Torridge), both of whom fell in love with her and wanted to marry her. As she had been away from home for a long time, her father became anxious and came to seek her. After a long search he heard the voices of the giants and found his daughter. He was furious and cast a spell

The source of the Tamar

on the two giants that sent them into a deep sleep. Tamara, however, would not return home, so in a fit of rage her father cursed her and changed her into a stream which flowed through the valleys growing into a river, now known as the Tamar.

When Tavy awoke he was dismayed to find Tamara gone; he quickly journeyed to the hills of Dartmoor where his father lived. Now the old giant, being a magician, knew what had taken place and felt deep sorrow for his son who he then changed into a stream and sent him off to find Tamara. Away went Tavy, rushing off the moor, over rocks, down valleys, until at last he met her. Later, when Tawridge woke up and discovered what had taken place he quickly sought out a magician and begged to be changed into a river. His request was granted, but in his eagerness he mistook the directions given to him and after rushing around madly, he turned northwards and now flows as the River Torridge into Bideford, North Devon.

The Tamar is not all that it seems, that is, being the river boundary between Cornwall and Devon. It rises on Woolley Moor, close to a minor road leading to East Youlstone Farm, off the A39 Atlantic Highway. Just over one mile away to the north rises the River Torridge, together with the border river to the north coast, Marsland Waters in close proximity. Cornwall on this high desolate moor land almost becomes an island.

The Tamar flows through Tamar Lakes that supply water to the surrounding area, from Hartland to Crackington Haven, but then a half mile downstream the boundary leaves the Tamar and Devon takes in a few square miles of Cornwall before returning to the river boundary to continue to the parish of Bridgerule; here the village straddles the Tamar. This presented the Boundary Commissioners in 1966 with a headache; the solution they came up with in order to have the Tamar as the border, was to split the village in half. This was strongly opposed by the villagers who were adamant the village should remain as one. They won the day; the village and parish boundaries remain the same and Devon extends into Cornwall. A few miles downstream, at least a third of North Tamerton parish intrudes into Devon, and so the interchange continues, but on reaching Werrington a substantiate decision was needed. For over 800 years the parishes of Werrington and North Petherwin, an area of over 12,000 acres were in Devon. We need to go back to the year 838 AD and what we now know as the final defeat of what historians call 'West Welsh' by Egbbert, followed by a 're-distribution of land'. During the Norman period, around 1086 AD the Abbey of Tavistock, then acquired the land which subsequently placed them firmly in Devon. Interestingly, the border of Cornwall and Devon was primarily the River Ottery (Attery) and a clear indication of that is in the place names. On the Cornwall side, a preponderance of Celtic place names and on the Devon side hardly any, as it was settled in the Saxon period. In 1894 the Boundary Commission recommended the area should be given to Cornwall (or returned I would have said) but the House of Lords in their wisdom rejected this saying "the boundaries of Wessex are immemorial". Again, the case was submitted and defeated by the Lords in 1929. However, the Boundary Commissioners finally had their day in 1966 and justice was achieved at last. Werrington and North Petherwin left Devon and Broadwoodwidger Rural District Council to once again play a role in Cornwall's affairs.

Tamar leaves the troubled political waters of its early journey to arrive at Polson Bridge, beneath Launceston for so long the bastion of power in Cornwall. Polson was not the earliest bridge to cross the Tamar, that honour falls to Bridgerule, where both river banks are in Devon. Here, we go back to the eleventh century, not long after the Norman Conquest. This was followed shortly afterwards by the building of Polson bridge and was to remain the principal point of entry into Cornwall for centuries. Re-built in 1852, it was eventually superseded by Dunheved Bridge in 1976 when the new A30 road was built around Launceston.

Here we leave the River Tamar and Tamara appropriately at the half way stage in its journey from north to south coast - a distance of some forty miles.

From a humble beginning the River Tamar starts its journey to the coast.

Calstock Viaduct over the Tamar

St Columb Major Church
A remarkable feature of the tower is the roadway which passes through it by means of open arches on the north and south sides.

Happenings in North Cornwall

THIS month let us look back at the period of the mid to late 1800s for a glimpse of life as it was in and around North Cornwall at that time.

A case of gluttony; here the correspondent assures us that a person who attended a sale at one of the local mines in this area, actually devoured the following quantity of refreshments at the dinner given to those in attendance: 4lbs of beef and mutton, 6 large potatoes, one cabbage, half a loaf of bread, 5 glasses of porter, 2 glasses of brandy, 6 glasses of white wine, 5 glasses of port, 16 glasses of grog and six plates of strawberries.

Yet the previous year a poor man named Alsop, living in St Austell with a wife and nine children and who had not been able to obtain work sufficient to provide the means of existence, whilst conveying coals in a wheelbarrow, for hire, fell through exhaustion and shortly expired. The unfortunate family were found in the most destitute condition and it was clearly proved that the unfortunate man had actually died from starvation!

This was the period in our history when the exodus of the Cornish families began; a report from Padstow reads: The race for emigration that now prevails in the north of this county is wholly unprecedented in Cornwall. In different parishes from two hundred to three hundred persons each, have departed or are preparing to leave for Canada or the United States. Last week a vessel named the Springflower, sailed from Padstow, having on board one hundred and eighty passengers and another, the Economist, is now ready for sailing with two hundred more. The recent regulation of the Privy Council, requiring that a regular medical practitioner be engaged for the voyage, in every vessel taking more than fifty passengers has caused some delay.

Cholera was the great fear of the time and at the first meeting of the Bodmin Board of Health, the following resolutions were adopted. *That in the pursuance of the Order of his Majesty's Council, already posted in the town, the borough and parish be divided into ten districts and inspectors attached to each. That it shall be the duty of the inspectors to examine all the houses, drains, sewers, courtyards and other places within the district where any dung filth is deposited and require the inhabitants or owners to remove the same within five days.* Horse drawn vehicles, known as Scavenger carts were used to take away all the ashes and filth each day.

The headline read 'Drowned in Delabole Quarry' – On Friday last, an inquest was held on the body of James Davey, who was drowned about three weeks since, by falling into a pool at Delabole slate quarry. The owner of the quarry refused to be involved with any expense in retrieving the body and the fellow workmen of the deceased were compelled to obtain pumps which they worked night and day until they succeeded in their objective.

The following month saw an explosion at St Tudy. On the evening of Tuesday the 27th whilst Mr Wright, a shopkeeper of St Tudy, was weighing some gun powder from a barrel for a customer, a spark from a candle fell on some loose grains on the counter, which communicated to the barrel, when the whole instantly exploded and blew up the roof and walls of the house. Mr Wright was so dreadfully scorched that his recovery is considered doubtful. His two children were most providentially saved by one of the wooden house beams falling across the bed in which they were, thus protecting them.

It could be said in this instance the hand of the man caused the explosion and the hand of God saved the lives of the children, but as to whose hand was involved in the following, who can say?

A correspondent reported the following: Before the discovery and general adoption of lightening conductor rods, most Cornish churches suffered great damage from thunderstorms. St Columb Major church is known to have been struck by lightning at least three times, in 1665, 1690 and 1775. On Sunday, January 6th 1895, soon after evensong had commenced, there was a brilliant flash which lit up the whole building and was followed by a loud explosion. The congregation, panic stricken, rushed out of the church. Considerable damage was done by the electrical fluid which, after striking the tower, went through the belfry and travelled along the nave. An eye witness described it as a ball of fire, sending out sparks. Some accounts refer to this as a meteorite. There does not appear to have been any injuries amongst the congregation.

The ringers, who were still in the belfry, suffered considerably. They were stunned and one of them fell over the railings into the church, a depth of twenty five feet, sustaining serious injuries to his head. The belfry was said to be in great confusion. This can be taken as an under statement. All the glass in the windows was smashed, the matting was torn, there was a hole fifteen inches in diameter in the wall and the floor was littered with plaster and stones. A slight explosion occurred near the gas meter, with the result that the flooring was set on fire; this fortunately was promptly extinguished. St Columb church tower is one of the towers of which the actual date of the building is known. It is mentioned in the will of Sir John Arundell dated 1483, where he bequeathed twenty pounds, a very considerable sum at that time for the 'new' work of the campanile and bells.

The Black Cat of Bodmin Moor

"ONLY when the last tree has died and the last river has been poisoned and the last fish has been caught will we realise we cannot eat money." (A Cree Indian saying)

High above the river valley, forest trees peered down; their steady march off the moor brought to a halt by an ancient Cornish hedge which snaked along the skyline. Amongst the branches of a huge, old beech tree, a large, black cat stretched languidly, lazily lifted one paw to scratch an ear, yawned, and then gazed down over the valley again. Suddenly, she stiffened. A car approached along the forestry track and parked in a scrubby area, close to the tree. The doors opened and out stepped two men. After much conversation and walking around, the rear car door was opened, a sheep's fleece dragged out and thrown near the hedge. Next, a cut-out model of a large crouching, black cat was placed on top of the hedge.

The setting of the sun, the darkness of the forest, and the crouching, yellow eyed black model cat, was all too much for the now very curious, very hungry cat, poised up the tree. Cautiously, she descended the trunk, wary of the camera flashes and with a low growl padded towards the hedge. In truth, no one could have left the scene more quickly. The car bounced down the uneven track, showering its contents out through the open rear door. The first real photograph of 'the Beast of Bodmin' lost in the mad rush to leave.

The next day, a tabloid newspaper published exclusive photographs, showing a cat on top of a hedge in the setting sun, together with the remains of a dead sheep. International experts who were brought in positively identified the animal and 'the Beast of Bodmin Moor' was born. There were others who scratched their heads and knew differently, but they were never asked. The cat, who was there, never had her picture taken. The farmer, who found a cut-out model of a large black cat with yellow eyes on top of a hedge, felt it prudent to make no fuss and as to the waterproof clothing and camera equipment lying around, well that was a matter that could be dealt with 'dreckly'.

A local policeman, who had studied the cat's movements for three years, certainly knew different and there was a wary respect between both of them. A male cat which had also frequented the area over the past few months, had now moved on, leaving her alone and pregnant.

That evening the cat left the forest, never to return. An afternoon, when television, with lights blazing, media photographers with zoom lenses descended on this quiet, lonely stretch of the moor was all too much. She would not return to give birth. On reaching the edge of the forest, she gave a cry of anguish that echoed out over the moor and resounded back. The policeman, sheltering amongst the old tin workings heard her cry and understood the terrible sadness behind it.

On leaving the trees and crossing the open moor, she was accompanied, from a distance, by an old, grey muzzled fox, whilst overhead silently flew an owl, ever alert, ever observant of the territory they regarded as their own. The cat would kill and consume as much as she wanted, which allowed the old fox, who had lost most of his teeth, to come along later and pick over the remains. For the three of them, life would never be the same again.

From the old tin workings, the policeman scanned the moor with night glasses picking her out as she crossed his line of vision. Although he knew she had picked up his whereabouts, he climbed slowly up the hill to continue watching her movements. Momentarily, the moon shone through to light up the landscape. Looking down, he watched her enter a stone circle, overlooking the valley. She turned around to face him; for several minutes neither moved, then from her came a sad, mournful cry that echoed down over the valley and out onto the moor. As he raised his arm in salute, the clouds swept in, followed by a solitary moonbeam racing over the moor to illuminate the circle with a brief flash of light. The cat swung around, eyes blazing, one paw raised, then, as the moonbeam raced on, she left the circle in one mighty bound, a dramatic farewell he would never forget.

An owl hooted down in the valley. Sweeping the hillside, he picked out the old fox, dejectedly plodding back. The policeman followed, both deep in their own thoughts.

The cat crossed the River Fowey, climbing the steep hillside, on around Dozmary Pool, Colliford Lake, ever westward, ever away from the noise and intrusion that had entered her world.

The driver, cocooned in his warm cab, high above the A30 with 38 tonnes of freight behind, distracted by early morning, mindless chatter on the radio, never realised he had hit the cat, never realised how close to short-term fame he had come.

The policeman was drinking a cup of tea, ready to book off duty, when the call came through "Could you go out and identify a large dead cat on the A30 near Lords Waste in the centre of the moor?" When he arrived there the cat was lying on the grass bank, hardly marked, a glancing blow from the speeding lorry had killed her instantly.

Suddenly a car pulled up, out jumped two men, who opened the rear door and brought out their cameras. The tabloid would write the final chapter as well. They offered to take the cat away, saying that a well known local inn on Bodmin Moor would like to put the cat on display in a glass case. They laughed, "The Beast of Bodmin Moor" alive or dead would be a great tourist attraction.

Despite their protests the policeman covered the cat in a blanket and placed her in the police van, she deserved better than that. He carried her close to the stone circle. It was hard work but he dug deep to bury her facing across the valley. When the last shovel of peaty soil was thrown on the grave he stood back, a silent prayer, then he reached for his jacket and left.

An owl swooped low over the mound of earth and an old fox, who stood watching throughout, slowly walked away.

The above is a fictional story that I wrote in February 1985 for the Bodmin Broadsheet. The following is fact - on two occasions I have seen large cats. The first on Exmoor in 1968 and the second on Bodmin Moor in February 2000. Both sightings were subsequently confirmed.

Dozmary Pool & Colliford Lake

What is 'Rinding'?

THE following interview from August 1960 gives an insight into a way of life that had gone back many generations and helped sustain the leather industry.

The Bodmin man, who had carried out the craft of rinding every year for over 50 years was Mr R J L Bellringer of West End, Bodmin, who explained rinding involves taking the bark from oak trees which is used in the process for tanning leather.

"For many years, up to about 1930 this was a regular business," he said, "but very few people do rinding now". His son, Mr Harold Bellringer of St Neot had taken over from him. "I can still rind a tree," he stated, "but I get a bit puffed climbing the hilly woods".

"Rinding is carried out with rippers (a chisel shaped iron with a wooden handle). In bygone days younger men climbed from the top of a five-staved ladder to the top of the trees, rinding the trees as they slipped down. The bark was then dried in the sun for about a week. When sufficiently dry it was bound up in faggots (bundles) about four feet long and weighed about half a hundredweight. They used to be bound with sticks cut in the woods, but nowadays baler cord is used," he said.

"The faggots are then put in ricks and kept there for a week or two, before being loaded and taken to the tannery where they are weighed on a weighbridge and stacked in sheds. The tanners grind the bark into small chips before processing it.

"Rinding starts about the middle of April and continues to the end of June. There is a pause for a week or so when the trees change from bud to leaf. Warm damp weather is best when there is plenty of sap".

His near neighbour, Mr Bill Harvey, then nearly eighty, remembered how bark used to be transported to the tannery by horses and wagons, leaving Bodmin in the evenings and travelling through the night arriving at Croggans Tannery, Grampound, early the next morning. Mr Bellringer recalled at that time bark fetched £4 to £5 per ton.

When the loads arrived at the tannery they would be inspected. Pieces of bark from the loads were broken off, if the bark snapped clean it was alright, but if it would only bend they were docked some money.

Mr Bellringer could remember many good times rinding with the gang and could recall many local people involved: Tom Laundry, Cardinham, Charlie Green, John Covell and his son, Jack, John Ead and his son, Reg, Jack Renals and his sons, Jim, Bob, Jack and Fred from Fletcher's Bridge, Jack Wherry, Bill and Frank Masters from Mount and Terry Oliver from Fletcher's Bridge

Men of Granite

MAN has used granite from early history to clear and enclose land, to build his round houses for ceremonial purposes out on the moor and for burial chambers; its use would encompass your whole life. For thousands of years the surface stone 'moorstone' was used and many partly worked examples can be seen today; one being on Showery Tor and Rough Tor. Search around and you will find a partly worked millstone which was discarded once a flaw developed. This must have been very frustrating as on average a millstone would take up to twenty days to complete. The winning of stone was and still is very hard physical work. The early method of splitting moorstone was done by driving in small iron wedges into chiselled slots. By the early 18th century an improved method was brought in called plug and feather. Splitting this involved drilling a series of holes into which iron plugs fitted with iron feathers, which were hammered in until the granite split. It was highly skilled work, of which much evidence can be seen today, but the returns were not high and every failure you might come across was extremely costly for the person involved.

The actual business of excavating and working a quarry is quite recent history. The requirement for good quality dimension stone by the mid 1800s saw the opening of the De Lank quarry at St Breward, which had the advantage of a good rail link, the Bodmin and Wenford Railway, to which they connected with an incline railway beneath St Breward. Transport was most important in these remote settlements when moving huge blocks of granite. The Minions Kilmar Tor and Bearah Tor on the east side of the moor developed its own railway to Moorswater, Liskeard and then onto Looe for shipping.

With the quarries came a new method of extracting granite, the use of gun powder. This again required a great deal of care and skill and enabled blocks to be moved within the quarry and for work to be carried out to completion.

The major granite quarries on Bodmin Moor have been in the west in the St Breward/Blisland area and the Minions area in the east. Today De Lank is the only major quarry still in production, with limited working at Tor Quarry and Bearah Tor. In the last century the quarries have had highs and lows, faced competition from abroad. Norway, in particular, was a keen rival and in an ironic twist, immediately after the two world wars, headstones and war memorials provided an increase in production. The first recorded despatch outside of Cornwall was from the Lanlivery district by the Treleaven brothers, Peter and Walter, who supplied granite for paving Westminster Bridge, as well as granite blocks for the Eddystone Lighthouse in 1706/09 and again for John Smeaton in 1756/59 shipped from the beach at Par, with difficulties I would think.

©PD

De Lank quarry supplied granite for the new Eddystone Lighthouse in 1881. Lighthouses, by their very nature, are built in dangerous places. The following, perhaps, gives a vivid picture of the dangers for those involved. 'The Smalls', a notorious reef with rocks extending for about three-quarters of a mile was a graveyard for sailing boats twenty miles from Solva on the Pembrokeshire coast and it was decided that a lighthouse was needed.

The resident engineer duly arrived at Solva Harbour in 1772 together with half a dozen Cornish miners, whose work was to pierce rock for insertion of pillars. On their first visit they only had time to fix in about four feet of a long iron bar before a strong southerly wind and an ugly sea caused their support vessel to leave them all clinging to this bar for three days and nights - it must have been terrifying. Despite this they carried on with the work, later on building huts for shelter, but these were also carried away and new ones had to be erected. There were times when the clothes of the workmen were torn to shreds by the waves and their skin lacerated by the sharp rocks. It was not for nothing that 'The Smalls' were regarded as the most inhospitable rocks in the United Kingdom. By 1835 it was decided to build a replacement lighthouse and to have the work completed by 1861. Sir James Nicholas Douglas, as resident engineer and twenty eight Cornish masons, with their families, all moved to Welsh speaking Solva, for the duration of the project. 3,696 tons of granite were imported from the

De Lank quarry on Bodmin Moor by sea and offloaded onto the quay, many weighing as much as eight tons. Here they were dressed and joints fashioned to interlock, then transported out to the reef. It was said on completion that the departure of the masons and their families was the occasion of many manifestations of regret by the inhabitants of Solva. The presence, for so long, of a busy 'hive' of lighthouse builders in a Welsh speaking village, reviving in such a wonderful manner, its almost stagnant trade.

Perhaps, a good illustration through to the completion, with all the hardships and with Wales, being hardly a giant's step away from Cornwall, I came across this story when we were on holiday in Pembrokeshire. My family originated from around Solva, three miles from St David's, at the far most tip of Wales and yes, my father was a Welsh speaker.

Bodmin Moor granite has been used for kerbing stones to massive projects, in this country and abroad. For instance, Beachy Head lighthouse, Blackfriars Bridge, Tower Bridge, Westminster Bridge in the 1950s, contracts for the Karl Marx memorial, pillars for the Magna Carta memorial at Runnymede and a granite statue of Lord Baden Powell. Others include; The British Museum, New Scotland Yard, Tate Gallery, Waterloo Station, Bombay Docks, Copenhagen Docks, Liverpool Docks and Singapore Docks, Portland Breakwater, Devonport Dockyard, the Stock Exchange and not forgetting of course, Bodmin Jail and the County Assize Courts building (now named Shire Hall) on Mount Folly. The prestigious list is endless.

Moorstone Bridge over the De Lank River, Bodmin Moor.

By kind permission of Peter Jewell

Edward Howard (Owie) Jewell, aged 88, Honoured Burgess of Bodmin, died in January 1992, a true son of Bodmin.

Edward Howard Jewell

EDWARD Howard Jewell was a self-made son of Bodmin who for half a century devoted his spare time to helping others and was known to one and all as 'Owie'. He lived in the town all his life like his father before him, left council school Robartes Road at the age of fourteen to work in a drapers' and men's outfitters and within a year joined Reeds Garage in Pound Lane as an apprentice motor engineer rising to clerk, salesman and manager, before leaving in 1936. He often said there was a wealth of knowledge to be learned from reading books and was living proof of that statement for during his time with Reeds he taught himself to be a radio engineer from books. Owie Jewell was very much one of the pioneers of radio in Cornwall, taking a keen interest when the first broadcasts began in the 1920s. This led to starting his own business from the garage office with his employer's blessing, needless to say!

The business grew quickly and in 1936 he branched out on his own, taking a shop in Fore Street and his son, Peter, until his retirement, proudly maintained the tradition of the company E H Jewell Ltd of Fore Street, Bodmin, just across the road from the original shop.

He was fortunate to have been supported throughout by his wife, Constance, and in 1986 they celebrated their diamond wedding, receiving a telegram from the Queen

Let us now look at his service to the town, as a result of the endless list of voluntary work Owie undertook, he was part of the backbone of Bodmin's community.

Owie was a founder member of Bodmin Rotary Club and served twice as President. In September 1988 he was made a Rotary Paul Harris Fellow, the highest honour that can be bestowed on an ordinary Rotarian in this country. He was a lifelong Freemason, he also helped to found the Bodmin Round Table and served as President. Owie was also a founder member of the Cornwall River Board on which he represented fishing interests from 1950 to 1963, a fitting association for a keen angler. Founder member and for many years, Owie was President of the Bodmin Angling Club. In 1919 he joined the St John Ambulance and just after passing his driving test was given charge of the Brigade's first motor ambulance, a converted First World War Buick. His commitment to the St John Ambulance was recorded in 1985 with his investiture as a serving brother during a special ceremony on St Michael's Mount. Between 1939 and 1964 he served as a special constable with the County Police Force at Bodmin and was known affectionately by many as 'The Chief of the Specials'; today his uniform is on display in Bodmin Town Museum.

Owie also had a very keen interest in local football, being a life member of the Town Football Club and its secretary from 1930 to 1947. He was President of the Bodmin and District Football League, a member of the Cornwall County Football Association and Referees' Association and President of the East Cornwall Football League and perhaps mention should be made of his wife, Constance, who washed the Bodmin Football kit for many years.

We continue with his involvement with the League of Friends of East Cornwall Hospital and Athelstan House, the Bodmin Scouts and Bodmin Gardening Association, both of which he had been president. The list continues with St Lawrence's Goodwill Club, Visually Handicapped and Over 60s clubs, Cornish Wrestling and so on.

In 1984 the distinction of Honoured Burgess – equivalent to Honorary Freeman in a Borough, was conferred upon him by Bodmin Town Council at a colourful ceremony in the Public Rooms, during which the Parish Church bell ringers rang a tribute peal and the Bodmin School Band played his favourite tunes 'Amazing Grace' and the 'Bodmin Riding Air'. Held in high regard by the people of Bodmin for his kindness and help over so many years the occasion was a joyful one and it was fitting, perhaps, that the Mayor was a Bodmin boy himself, Keith Searle.

For me 'Owie' had precious gifts, certainly humility, certainly a ready wit, certainly a sense of duty, combined with a great love of Bodmin.

I was fortunate to be welcomed into Owie's home on a number of occasions and whilst we sipped a glass of sherry he would reminisce over many stories of times past. Owie knew my interest and involvement with local football and the conversation would often come around to memories about Bodmin Town Football Club. The following was told to me on one of those visits which I feel is a fitting epitaph:-

Owie was secretary of Bodmin Town Football Club in the 1930s which was then situated for a while at ground near Barn Lane. Owie manned the gate, it poured with rain, two spectators paid, one demanding his money back at half time because he was soaked to the skin and the game was terrible anyway. Owie thought he was quite right in his thinking, gave him 3d back, put in 3d from his own pocket so the takings were 6d and it only looked half bad. Bodmin lost and Owie spent the next two weeks in bed with influenza.

Memories of a Cornish Childhood - One Hundred Years Ago

IN 1983, at the age of 75, Catherine Richards sat down and wrote of her childhood; as she put it from birth to the age of fourteen. So, here in her own words are her memories of another age.

Grace Cory Collection

Kate Eddy (nee Richards) in 1946.

I was born at my grandmother's house (that's my mother's mother) at Blowing House Hill, Trenance, St Austell on November 27th 1908.

My first memory was at the age of three when I went outside in the road and there was a white river running alongside. A little way down the road was a little bridge, which was a pathway to a blacksmith's shop. One day I was curious to see the river under the bridge, so I lay on my tummy – what happened? I fell in and the blacksmith caught me with his tongs. I was put in a warm bath and put to bed. When it got dark my mother gave me a candle to light up the bedroom. Being mischievous I took the candle and tried to look out the window and in doing so caught the curtains on fire. I was punished severely for that.

After a time we moved from my grandmother's house and went to live in a village called Penwithick, as my father was working at the clay works.

Then we moved to Bodmin. War was declared in 1914, so, of course, my dad had to join the army. I had two brothers and a sister by this time. Our cottage had a cellar and when dad came home on leave I used to hide down there so I would not see him go away again. Also, in this cellar the other children in the street used to join us and we would hold concerts down there. On Wednesday and Saturday evenings the Salvation Army used to make a ring and played their band and sang hymns and prayed under the gas lamp, which we loved. The gas man used to come around with a long pole and make the lights go out at 9.00pm.

As we lived near the Bodmin Jail we often used to see sailors being escorted to prison for doing something they shouldn't – like being drunk and disorderly. Some hangings had taken place at the prison but I didn't know very much about them.

My day school was situated near to the Bodmin Beacon. My Sunday school was quite near my house, so I went there mornings, afternoons and again in the evening; I also went to the chapel sometimes, where I used to sit in the choir. The chapel organ that accompanied us was worked by a man blowing bellows throughout the service. Every August bank holiday I used to go, with the other Sunday school children, to Polzeath; travelling in horse drawn carriages called wagonettes. When we came to a hill we had to get out and walk to the top. With Bodmin having the Barracks, there were a lot of soldiers to be entertained; so our Sunday school was called 'The Soldier's Rest'. We used to entertain them and provide tea and food. We used to go picking blackberries to make jam for the soldiers and we were paid so much a lb for them; we also used to go to the institute to help knit socks for the soldiers.

On one occasion, when my father came home on leave, I was very excited because he brought me a new coat; this was a big luxury for me.

In the spring, on Saturday afternoons, my friends and I used to go picking primroses and white violets at Bodiniel and Clerkenwater; we had to pass Bodmin Jail on the way and it was very scary. One afternoon we went for a walk to the top of a steep hill near the cemetery; we had a terrible fright as a Zeppelin airship came roaring past in the sky and one little girl actually died of shock - it was the first time anyone had seen a Zeppelin.

During the war years my mother had another little boy, so we called him Alec, as he was born on Alexandra Rose Day – June 23rd.

In 1918 peace was declared and there was great excitement. I remember going to the railway station to see the all of the troops coming home. I was ten years old when this happened; we all had flags and were presented with a mug. My grandmother, on my father's side, lived in Bugle and sometimes my dad would hire a pony and jingle and take us to visit her.

When the war was over my dad went back to his old job and was made Captain at the clay works at Bodmin Road, so we moved from Bodmin to Bodmin Road to live. My brothers, sisters and I went to the little two roomed school at Respryn, about a mile and a half away, within the Lanhydrock Estate. Mother used to come part of the way to meet us some dinner times bringing hot pasties for us to eat. Respryn is a small hamlet,

3 miles from Bodmin, nestling in the lovely valley of the River Fowey.

The church Sunday school was held at the Gatehouse (the former hunting lodge) which had a fascinating circular stairway. The children of the estate workers attended and afterwards went on to the church to take up their seats behind the entrance door, whereas the Robartes family entered by their own door at the top of the steps from their living quarters in Lanhydrock House. From the footpath to the church you could look into the dairy and see the pans of milk, with lovely crusted cream over the top. At home, Sundays were always special – we had 'Sunday tea' which consisted of pasties, egg and bacon pies, trifles and cakes.

I was very happy at Respryn School, leaving at the age of fourteen and spending my last August holiday working at the vicarage. Then it was time for me to move to St Austell to start full time work. My childhood was over.

IN 1902 a local paper published *'2s Every Girl Should Learn'*. I pass no comment only to say that five years later the movement for Women's Suffrage became active in Britain.

2 sew,

2 cook, 2 mend,

2 be gentle, 2 value time,

2 dress neatly, 2 keep a secret, 2 be self-reliant,

2 respect old age, 2 avoid idleness, 2 darn stockings,

2 make good bread, 2 keep a house tidy, 2 make home happy,

2 be above gossiping, 2 control her temper, 2 take care of the sick,

2 sweep down cobwebs, 2 take care of the baby,

2 humour a cross old man, 2 marry a man for his worth,

2 read the very best of books, 2 keep clear of trashy literature,

2 take plenty of active exercise, 2 be a helpmate to your husband,

2 be light-hearted and fleet-footed,

2 wear shoes that won't cramp the feet,

2 be a womanly woman under all circumstances.

Aerial view of St. Tudy Village (August 1995)
By kind permission of Charlie David, Cornwall Council's Countryside Service

Another famous person from the parish was Admiral William Bligh 1754 - 1817, a man destined to be remembered through the film "Mutiny on the Bounty" rather than one of the great navigators in history. The regrettable result of the film is you are left thinking of Bligh as a cruel and sadistic captain who enjoyed nothing more than having his men flogged. It is true Bligh had his faults, including a fiery temper, but the mutiny on the Bounty was more likely brought about by his obstinate courage and determination to carry out Admiralty orders, than to senseless tyrannical conduct. He served his country faithfully, but it would be many years before he cleared his name.

St Tudy Man Pioneered Blood Transfusion

CORNWALL was rich in small squires who built themselves manor houses of slate and granite on wooded slopes, out of the wind and near a stream, from the 15th and 16th centuries onwards. No Cornish parish contains more small squires' houses than the undulating and luxuriant series of valleys between the Allen and Camel rivers wrote the late John Betjeman in 1964 when viewing the parish of St Tudy. He considered the church town of the village to be a pleasant scatter of cottages and contains a handsome rectory of stone by Edmund Sedding 1909 in a strong and simple arts and craft style.

Today the village centre is within a conservation area which fortunately helps it to remain one of the most attractive villages in North Cornwall. Let us now consider a historical landmark in surgery that has a St Tudy connection - the transfusion of blood, which plays such a vital part in modern hospital practice. We talk familiarly today of Blood Groups, Blood Donors and Blood Banks, and tend to think of Blood Transfusion as a relatively modern marvel of surgery. As a matter of fact, it had its beginnings more than 300 years ago.

It is not generally known that a Cornishman was one of the first to perform a blood transfusion. He was Richard Lower, born in 1631 at Tremeere, St Tudy. Dr Lower was educated at Westminster School. He graduated at Christchurch, Oxford, studying medicine and obtaining both MA and MD degrees; later becoming an assistant in a large London practice. On the death of the senior partner, Richard Lower assumed the leading position. According to the famous diarist Samuel Pepys, the Cornish born doctor was esteemed the most noted physician in Westminster and London, and no man's name was more cried up in Court than his.

For several years Dr Lower 'physician and physiologist' was one of a remarkable group of Oxford medical men whose original researches paved the way for some of today's achievements.

His own contribution to the team work at Oxford related mainly to the heart and circulation of blood, he was also described as a 'medical writer of high standing'. Pepys's diary tells of Doctor Lower's most remarkable 'experiment' - that of transferring blood direct from one dog into the veins of another in 1666; there was a pretty experiment of the blood of one dog let out (till he died) into the body of another on one side while all his own run out on the other side. The first died upon the place, and the other very well and likely to do well.

As to be expected there was much public controversy about the case. A Cambridge Professor said, "If it takes, it may be a mighty use to man's health for the amending of bad blood from a better body." With Dr Lower being a Quaker it did lead to some facetious remarks, as Pepys wrote; "It did give occasion to many pretty wishes, as of the blood of a Quaker to be let into an Archbishop and such like".

Just a year later Arthur Coga, a man healthy in blood but somewhat simple in mind, submitted himself to the operation. In his case the blood of a sheep was let into his body, about 12 ounces or a flow of blood for exactly one minute. Coga's fee was twenty shillings and a few days afterwards he declared himself, "much better and as a new man and willing to have the same again". Pepys records that this was the first authentic case in England, but a Paris surgeon claimed to have performed the operation on a boy using lamb's blood the year before. The boy was said to have made a good recovery, but if that was true it was more by luck than skill, for animal blood is incompatible with human blood.

Other such trials were made, but with so many fatal consequences that various European governments banned the practice of transfusion and it lapsed for nearly two centuries. It could not have succeeded until the compatibility and blood groups were understood, and it was the two World Wars of the last century which advanced the research needed.

On a January night in 1690, Dr Richard Lower's house chimney caught fire and he stayed so long extinguishing it, he developed a fever which killed him in a few days. He was buried at St Tudy. It is high praise which modern text books record of him. Modern research gives him higher credit for his work in anatomy and physiology than was originally assigned to him.

Today's article was prompted by the arrival through the letterbox of an invite to the next blood donor session. I have donated blood since 1964, could you donate as well? That one simple move could save a life.

Through the Looking Glass reveals the families' history

WHEN Bodmin Town Museum received two fragments of glass brought in for possible identification, they revealed a valuable insight into a period when the leather trade was very important to local commerce and a source of considerable employment. Glass fragment 'A' had the personal seal on what had been an eighteenth century wine bottle embossed with P Deacon Bodmin 1775.

WHJ

Research found evidence regarding the owner of the bottle. Philip Deacon, who was not born in Bodmin, married Martha. There are two christening records: Elizabeth Deacon – 25/9/1758 and Philip Deacon 14/1/1761 who were both born in Bodmin. It seems very likely that the owner of the bottle was the father of these children, although the Christening records show no trade or profession for the father. Further documentation from the National Archives shows that he was a tanner and a landowner.

At that time during the tanning process the hides from cattle were thoroughly washed and then steeped in limewater to facilitate the removal of hair. It is recorded of Tower Hill tannery that squeamish people were continually objecting to the odour from the lime yard there. The next stage in the process was the tanning and tree bark rind *(see 'Rinding', Page 72)* from oak trees, was milled to obtain tannic acid to convert the hides into leather. I have read that dog faeces and urine were collected and used; that being the case it is little wonder that people complained about the smell. The tanning process required a fell-monger, who had prepared the hides for the tanner who then worked the hides for the curriers, who dressed tanned hides for the leather workmen.

For Philip Deacon this was a very busy period as leather was now in high demand. Horses were then the motive power used for agricultural work, mining and as the roads improved so did the requirements for horse drawn coaches, making the saddle and harness trade skilled work. The occupation of cordwainers (boot and shoe makers) thrived in Bodmin, numbering 101 of these craftsmen by 1831.

WHJ

Glass fragment 'B' had a personal seal and it was embossed Jos Eyre Bodmin. In the Parish Baptism records for Bodmin, the name Eyre appears 47 times between 1740 and 1837. Some fathers' trades are recorded as Tawers (they converted skins into white leather), Woolstaplers, Feltmongers and Victuallers. Other members of the family included Thomas and John 1742 to 1774, Keepers of the County Bridewell Prison. A report of the period informs *'the County pays £10 per year for this prison. It is much out of repair and the walls around the yard not safe enough to let the prisoners use it. The night rooms are two garrets, with small windows. Keepers' salary lately raised from £20 to £28 per annum'.* Thomas and John were also 'Grain Inspectors' for regulating the importation and exportation of grain, a responsible appointment. But, as always when you delve into family history a black sheep appears and here we have Joseph Eyre in 1774 – Bastardy case in Breage. Father being proven as Joseph Eyre of Bodmin, maintenance and lying-in costs awarded. 1781 – Joseph Eyre committed to Bridewell as vagrant. Surely not the same man with the private bottle seal! He was only 18 in 1774.

My thanks to Dr Bill Johnson for the supply of the research material.

Please use your local museums in North Cornwall; we are there to help with local history and take pleasure in doing so. North Cornwall museums are found in Bodmin, Bude, Launceston, Padstow and Camelford. Wadebridge has also recently formed a new museum.

I can assure you all are well worth visiting.

Al Hodge - he struck a chord for Cornwall

By kind permission of Pam Hodge

IN July 2006, Cornwall lost one of its greatest guitarists/singers/ composers. Al Hodge was unique. He was as much at home playing the pubs and clubs he loved in Cornwall as he was on the world stage.

When Al was about 10 years old, his father, Arthur, used to take him along to watch and at times, play, with *The Gunslingers,* a popular Bodmin band (Frank Cory, Rick Surtees, Elliot Osborne, Mike Blackborrow, Pete Lawry and Pete Ellis). Even at this young age Al was able to surpass their guitar playing.

His talent and confidence was first recognised at the age of 13 during a music festival at the Bodmin Secondary School in 1963 when performing the Shadows' instrumental 'Foot Tapper', solo, in front of the whole school. He then joined a Bodmin-based beat group called *'The Jaguars'* as lead guitarist. The Jaguars were jointly managed by Al's father, Arthur Hodge and Tony Webb, whose son Cliff played rhythm guitar in the band. The other members were Rob Hancock (bass), Dennis Phillips (Fritz) on Drums plus Tony Priest and David Thompson (vocalists).

Al was a perfectionist and the Jaguars became so popular and successful that in their first year they won the Cornish Beat Group Championships at Truro City Hall against strong opposition. *The Jaguars* were offered the chance to turn professional but all refused except Al, who went on to join the popular West Country band - *The Onyx.* They toured the UK and Europe in the sixties with regular appearances on BBC Radio One and recording 7 singles on the Pye label.

In 1970 Al came back to Bodmin and joined *the Ginhouse,* whose members included Tony (Dick) Gynn, John Pearn, Bill Gill, Paul Thomas, Nick Floyd, Brian Searle, Derek Fitzpatrick and Colin 'Broccoli' Brokenshire.

The Ginhouse will be fondly remembered by many locals who enjoyed their regular gigs at the TA Centre and the Public Rooms.

In 1971 Al joined the Sawmills Studio in Golant as a session musician where, in 1978, the *Mechanics* were formed and became a prominent rock group worldwide, with Al Eden (drummer and studio man) and Dave Quinn (bass), with Steve Jackson taking over as drummer in 1982.. In 1980 the Mechanics teamed up with Leo Sayer and two world tours followed.

As well as playing with some of the greatest pop and rock musicians in the business, including Elkie Brooks, Suzi Quatro, Toyah Willcox, Sad Café, Randy Crawford and Clifford T Ward to name but a few, Al wrote many fine pieces of music. These ranged from full-on rock to beautiful ballads and from orchestral pieces to the music for the theatrical production at the Hall for Cornwall of the D M Thomas's book 'Hellfire Corner', the story of the legendary Cornish rugby player, Bert Solomon.

Mention should be made of his faithful road crew - Paul Woodhams and Darren White (sound), Roger Butler (lights) and technical 'Visor' Jumbo (alias Brian Chapman) whose contribution over the years was considerable.

In more recent times Al had joined the Cornwall Music Service and taught the guitar to dozens of music students. John Pearn, life long friend who joined the Jaguars when Al left, pays the following tribute:

"Al was a natural teacher - wonderfully talented, inspirational and great fun. Apart from his catalogue of music, one of Al's most valuable legacies will be the knowledge that he has passed on to many young guitar players. If any of those young players make it big in the ephemeral world of modern pop music, they will owe a big debt to Al Hodge".

Big Al Hodge lost his fight against a brain tumour on Thursday 13th July 2006 at Bodmin Hospital. He was a wonderful person, loving husband to Pam and devoted father to Jodie and Luke. His funeral took place at St Petroc's Church with the wake being held at Bodmin Football Club, over which the flag of St Piran had been lowered to half-mast. The function room at the Football Club, which Al felt was his second home, has recently been renovated and renamed 'Big Al's Bar' to commemorate Bodmin's musical legend.

My sincere thanks to Grace Cory and John Pearn who have helped in the research for this article.

Sandercock of the Yard

DETECTIVE Inspector 'Joe' Sandercock retired from police service special branch in 1922 and during his twenty years as a detective officer he became one of the most well known figures at Scotland Yard; held in high regard by all who knew him.

He came from an old established Bodmin family; his father was a foreman mason, a man dedicated to his work that included the building of the Public Rooms in 1891, the restoration of St Petroc's Parish Church and tower, the erection of the DCLI depot and served with contractors for the new railway viaducts in the Liskeard area.

From the small county town of Cornwall 'Joe' Sandercock travelled to the capital of England, London, where he was eventually to become one of the most formidable police detectives of the early 20th century.

Wartime Spy-tracker. It is said that during the 1st World War that Sandercock was credited, both directly and indirectly, with the capture and ultimate execution of more spies than any other single officer. He was stationed at Antwerp and Harwich during the war. He was also responsible for the safety of the King, the Empress of Russia, the King and Queen of Spain, the King of Greece, the King of Denmark, Lloyd George and Winston Churchill. He had an extensive knowledge of languages and was sent on special enquiries to Greece, Holland and other countries. On one occasion, during a General Election, he paid an official visit to Bodmin accompanying Winston Churchill, who spoke in the Market House.

He received an honour from His Majesty the King of Greece, who conferred upon him the Cross of the Chevalier of the Order of George I, in recognition of the valuable services rendered by him during the war.

The Inspector was one of the very best; as well as one of the most popular of old-time detectives. His biggest case concerned Roger David Casement, a prominent Irish Nationalist, who was hanged at Pentonville Prison in 1916 for high treason, following the Easter Rising in Ireland. During the trial Mr Sandercock used to take Casement from the prison in the morning and back again in the evening by means of taxicabs. Casement knew his end was certain, long before the trial had finished, and once said to Mr Sandercock, "Well, Inspector, I will not see much more of London. Do you mind going a different way back to the prison today, so that I can see as much of the town as possible?" Mr Sandercock granted this request. So, following each day's proceedings at the Court he drove the prisoner around London. Once when Casement said the only thing he longed for was a bottle of stout, the Inspector said, "You will get me the sack before you have finished, but come along, you shall have one". Mr Sandercock actually stopped the taxicab outside a public house, took the prisoner inside and bought him a drink, after which he conducted him back to jail.

Casement wrote a letter to Sandercock, in which he stated, I want to thank you very warmly and most sincerely for your unfailing courtesy, manliness and kindness to me. From the time you took me in custody at Euston station and to the Tower of London, you showed me the best side of an Englishman's character - his native good heart.

He arrested Irving Guy Ries, who was in this country ostensibly on a mission from New York to sell compressed cattle foods but was in fact a spy in the employ of the Germans. Ries, who stayed at the best hotels in the country and who apparently enjoyed life to the full, was in the early hours of one morning interrogated by Mr Sandercock at one of London's premier hotels. Ries declared that he was an American citizen, born in Chicago, and although Mr Sandercock found nothing incriminating in his belongings, he arrested him.

It was proved that Ries was not a genuine commercial traveller, that his American passport had been forged and that he had been sending valuable information, by means of invisible ink, to the Germans. He worked through a notorious woman spy whose headquarters were in Rotterdam. Ries was found guilty of espionage and sentenced to death by firing squad within the Tower of London.

When the suffragist movement was at its height, he was sent to guard Mr Lloyd George (then Chancellor of the Exchequer) and Mr Winston Churchill. On one occasion Mr Lloyd George had been addressing a meeting at Caxton Hall, Westminster. They were leaving in a motor car when a heavy object struck the window. Mr Sandercock found that a heavy iron bound attaché case had been hurled and narrowly missed the minister's head. Later he had the satisfaction of arresting the person who threw the bag.

He used to tell of an exciting encounter he had with a man who attempted to lash Mr Churchill with a whip; again, it was during the suffragist unrest. Mr Churchill and the Inspector were in the train travelling from Bradford when a burly man in the same carriage suddenly pulled a whip from his coat. The Inspector was too quick for the assailant and swiftly overpowered and arrested him. The Inspector was always handy with his fists and often had to defend himself, to the consternation of anyone trying to attack him.

Cornish policeman of the era: PC 72 Maurice Light, Cornwall County Constabulary. Joined the force on 25th February 1893. Specially commended by the Secretary of State re work with aliens during the 1914-18 war. Born at St Neot in 1871 and married Bessie Congdon of Dobwalls in 28 April 1895.

In January 1911, a party of alien Russian gangsters, led by a Russian anarchist, namely Jacob Peters, known as 'Peter the Painter' tried to raid a London jeweller's shop and shot and killed three policemen who interrupted them. They were traced to a house in Sidney Street and were then surrounded by a police cordon. But, when an attempt was made to arrest them, they shot and killed another constable. This was now the so-called Sidney Street siege, made all the more famous by the arrival of Winston Churchill, Home Secretary, who had felt it important to hurry to the scene and supervise operations.

At his side throughout the incident, was Mr Sandercock. The military were appealed to and Scots Guards came along from the Tower of London, erected a barricade at the end of the street and opened fire on the house. It was an exciting occurrence in those peaceful days for a real war to break out in London with a gang of bandits armed with automatic pistols, shooting police and fighting soldiers. Crowds assembled at vantage points and looked on enthralled by the spectacle. A field gun was brought in to reinforce the attack and eventually the house was set ablaze. Peter the Painter, himself, managed to elude the police cordon and get away, only to reappear years later in other dubious circumstances, but the corpses of his associates were found in the smouldering ruins of the house when the blaze subsided.

Detective Inspector Joseph Sandercock of Special Branch, Scotland Yard, a Cornishman, was a truly remarkable policeman who deserved all the accolades given him at the time of his retirement.

Private James Henry Finn VC - His townsfolk did not forget

ON Remembrance Sunday 13th November 1966 the heroism of a young Bodmin private soldier who won the Victoria Cross 50 years before and who died before he could receive the medal, was remembered.

The name of the man singled out for this special honour was Pte James Henry Finn and before the remembrance Parade took place a £120,000 housing estate, built on the site of the Finn family home in Downing Street, was named after him, Finn VC Estate.

Pte Finn was born in Truro, but lived in Bodmin from a young age, attending the Council school at the top of Robartes Road. On leaving school he travelled to South Wales to find employment. He found work in a colliery in Abertillery and it was there, at the outbreak of war, he enlisted in the South Wales Borderers. Within two years he was fighting the Turks in Mesopotamia.

The story of Private Finn's heroism

The official account issued in connection with the award, telling the story of Private Finn's courageous deed is as follows: *After a night attack, he was one of a small party dug in at the front of our advanced line, about 300 yards from the enemy trenches. Seeing several wounded men lying out in front, he went out and bandaged them all under heavy fire, making several journeys in order to do so. He then went back to our advance trench for a stretcher and being unable to get one, he, himself carried a wounded man to safety. He then returned and was aided by another man, who was wounded during the act, carried in another badly wounded soldier. He was under continuous fire while performing this gallant work.*

It was not the first engagement in which he had rendered conspicuous service. However, in May of the previous year (1915) he was recommended for honourable mention in connection with a very courageous action, risking his life in bringing in his wounded company officer.

A letter sent to his father dated 17th June 1917 reads as follows:

Dear Mr Finn,

I cannot tell you how sorry I am that you have not before received particulars from the Regiment of the death of your very gallant son, Private J. H. Finn, V.C. I should have written to you myself had I been there, but at that time I was in hospital in India, having been wounded earlier in the operations and I did not hear of your son's death until my return a short time ago. He was wounded in the leg during a fight on March 29th, on Noel Plane, about 50 miles north of Baghdad. His Company Commander got a stretcher party to take him back to the Field Ambulance, but on the way he was struck again by a bullet in his side. It was this wound that proved fatal.

General Lavin told me that he went to the ambulance and saw your son, who was at that time not suffering much, but seemed to know his end was near. He was buried near the ambulance. I am sorry not to be able to give you a sketch of the grave, but the position has been marked and later on it may be possible to do this. At present the grave is outside our Outpost line and some miles from our present position.

It was a great blow to hear of your son's death as I was very proud of him, he having been my servant for a good many months last year. His devotion to the wounded was remarkable and I know that he has saved many lives by rendering first aid to his wounded comrades. He has shown absolute contempt of danger when under fire and was always ready and anxious to do anything to help anyone and we shall badly miss him in the Regiment. I expect he told you that he was awarded a Serbian Decoration – the Gold Medal – before he was killed.

He added lustre to the record of his Regiment. We are all very proud of him and shall reverence his memory. May I express to you and his family our very deepest sympathy for you in your sorrow.

Believe me, yours very sincerely,

C. E. KITCHEN, Lt Col.,

Commanding 4th South Wales Borderers.

In 1954 his mother presented his Victoria Cross to the town of Bodmin, together with his other medals, which include the Order of Karageorge, the Serbian equivalent of the V.C. and following the ceremony his family presented further items including his diary.

In response to a letter from Lorna Warden of Lanivet in the NCA's November edition with regards to Private James Henry Finn VC Memorial Fund, I hope the following will be of interest.

There was a presentation in the Bodmin Guildhall in 1918 to the family and on the stage was an enlarged framed portrait of Pte. Finn VC which was to be hung in the Free Library. A marble clock was also presented to the family with an inscription, together with medals on display.

Mr Randall, treasurer of the subscription fund, reported that a total of £3215.6s.9d. was raised and that the balance of £3200 was invested in war stock bearing 5% interest. It was proposed the balance would pay for X-ray equipment in 1921 at the East Cornwall Hospital when it would be required. It was agreed the money subscribed should, in the main, be devoted to the ministry of healing. Pte. Finn had won the Victoria Cross in trying to save life and nothing could be more appropriate as a memorial.

1st July 1921 saw two ceremonies; the first being at the Free Library with the unveiling of the war memorial followed by a procession to the East Cornwall Hospital to dedicate the X-ray equipment. Prior to the purchase of the equipment a suitable building was required and Miss Agar-Roberts was kind and generous in having this erected for them at the rear of the hospital.

Bodmin Town Museum has a copy of the portrait of Pte. Finn together with a display of artefacts.

Should you visit Wales and the town of Brecon you will find the museum has also acknowledged the bravery of Pte. Finn who served in the South Wales Borderers, a very brave young man indeed.

James Henry Finn V.C., an exceptionally brave young man, died at the age of 23.

Umbrellas and Statistics could lead to Beer and Happy Days

I MUST admit at times my thoughts do dwell on the subject of rain and if we are honest with one another so do yours as well; we live in Cornwall with its wonderful lush, green landscape.

However, if we go back sixty years to 1946, we would have found the Chief Constable of Cornwall, Major Hare, also pondering, not about the lack of rainfall, but the amount that deposited itself on his Castle Hill house and the parish of Bodmin, during a very wet twenty-four hours.

The Eye Well adjacent to Dennison Road car park had a reputation for healing weak and troubled eyes as well as supplying water for the local inhabitants.

You see, Major Hare was a man who kept meticulous records about the weather in the borough and following that wet weekend, sat down with a pen and paper and eventually arrived at the following: Bodmin's rainfall during the twenty-four hours ending Monday 12th August was 1.72 inches, the heaviest for the year. As one inch of rainfall gives 100.9 tons to the acre, Bodmin's 3,312 acres received about 575,000 tons of rain during the twenty-four hour period from Sunday to Monday. This, as near as he could estimate it, would give an overflowing 22,000 gallons to every man, woman and child of the population in the borough. Mind you, it was a very wet year, although in 1946 with a total rainfall of 60.91 inches with rain on 223 days, the average rainfall for Bodmin is 46 inches, so if you were a shopkeeper selling umbrellas, you would have had a very good year.

Now, in response to the above, a gentleman from Bodmin presented another statistic relating to the same twenty-four hours that may mean more to some than others. For you see 1946 was a dry year, yes there was a shortage of beer; hence the following flowed from the pen. 'If it had rained beer during the twenty-four hours, not only would the shortage be settled for all times, but it would allow for seven and a half pints per day for every man, woman and child in the town during an average life span of a 75 years lifetime.' 'Happy Days'.

When describing rain in the borough, the 1903 official guide has a delightful way with words that surely could not cause offence. Rainfall is somewhat abundant, but this replenishes the sparkling springs and streams and causes no permanent inconvenience. The climate of Bodmin is bracing, but mild. There are no swamps or stagnant ditches and scarcely any marshy ground. The ground is nearly everywhere on an incline. Water therefore does not lie on the surface.

The town leat, behind the buildings (left), overflowed. Flooding the platform and track in the Southern Railway yard (1936).

So, there we are, rainfall is somewhat abundant but causes no permanent inconvenience - we must remember that next time it rains.

The Amateur - The Professional - and a Drop of Brandy

THE very word 'dentist' can conjure up all sorts of fears and phobias in even the most strong willed of us, yet the practice of dentistry can be traced back to Ancient Egypt as early as 3700BC. After the fall of the Roman Empire, the Arabs were using gold to fill tooth cavities, and moving forward again to the medieval period in Europe it was the monks who carried out most of the dental work. It was not until the late Victorian era that the situation began to change from perhaps your local blacksmith or enthusiastic amateur within the community to a doctor willing to carry out the work.

Mr W J P Burton, at the age of 79 years, recalled in a talk he gave in Bodmin in 1936 of a character called 'Cap'n Hambly' who was an enthusiastic amateur. Cap'n Hambly was an old retired naval officer who resided in Bodmin in the mid to late 1800s when there was no qualified dentist in the town. The doctors were usually resorted to for the extraction of troublesome teeth for a fee, but there were one or two amateurs who operated 'for the love of the thing'. Cap'n Hambly was one of these and the story is told of a man who had been awake all night with an aching tooth and called upon a friend in the early morning to go with him to Cap'n. It was not lack of courage that the sufferer called upon his friend but that his friend happened to be a familiar acquaintance of the Cap'n while the man with the aching tooth was not.

It was Sunday morning and the Cap'n did not mind being disturbed. The forceps got hold of the tooth and the man in the chair gave a frightful yell and struggled to get to his feet. However, the Cap'n held him down and the tooth was removed. When they emerged to the street outside the friend asked why he had made such a fool of himself struggling and yelling in the chair. Silently the poor victim opened his mouth and pointed to his bleeding tongue, from which a portion had been removed with the offending tooth.

By the 1890s people were undertaking training to become dentists and Cornwall was not left behind. One of the first was William Henry Lyne, born 10th December 1871 and raised in Launceston. He qualified as a dental surgeon in 1893 and set up practice in Liskeard, probably being one of the first in Cornwall and was very successful.

Kelly's Directories for 1914 and 1919 record dental businesses in Liskeard, Looe, Bodmin, West Bowithick, St Clether, Altarnun and Launceston. During the First World War he would travel from Liskeard on his motor cycle to visit his two daughters, who were working as land girls at Bowithick on the north side of Bodmin Moor. On the way he would pull teeth from farm workers who were aware of his journey that day and sat in the field hedges alongside the roads to await his arrival and an end to an aching tooth.

William Lyne was a Methodist lay preacher for sixty years and lived out his days in the far west of Cornwall, where he had again continued to provide dental services to people in their homes and found himself 'called up' to provide dentistry in Penzance during the second World War at the age of nearly seventy.

OLD FALSE TEETH BOUGHT.

Have you any old false teeth by you ? Why not turn them into Money ? R. D. & J. B. Fraser, Princes Street, Ipswich (Estd. 1833), buy old false teeth. If you send your teeth to them they will remit you by return of post the utmost value; or if preferred, they will make you the best offer, and hold the teeth over for your reply. If reference necessary, apply to Messrs. Bacon & Co., Bankers, Ipswich.

In the western world, during medieval times, the population did not have good teeth, with gum problems and tooth decay – a prominent example being Queen Elizabeth I, who was said during her reign to have blackened stumps for teeth. For ordinary people and travellers, bread was a staple part of their diet and the local miller played an important role as badly ground flour could cause a great deal of damage, including chipped teeth and a visit to the village blacksmith, who performed the extractions, was often needed. We have learned through the writings of historians and educated people of that time that portrait artists, painting to their clients' purse, would be in mortal danger if they completed a picture of a young woman with rotting teeth and warts.

For instance, what is really behind the serene smile of 'Mona Lisa' by Leonardo de Vinci (1452-1519) or 'The Laughing Cavalier' by Frans Hall (1582-1666) - not laughing but with lips drawn quite tightly, more of a smirk, or is this being unduly cynical?

For many with pain or illness, particularly country folk, would rely upon the faith and treatment that had come through generations of charmers and faith healers who built up a vast knowledge with handed down cures for the treatment of body and mind. Farmers would welcome a visit to their sick animals when herbal remedies or charms would be used and were for the most part, successful. Cornwall, with its poor roads and

lack of communication were reliant on these gifted people who carried out a lot of good work and still do today.

There are other remedies for pain and suffering, as related in the book by the late curator of Bodmin Museum, Leslie Long 'An Old Cornish Town' under the headline 'The Revival'. Three men were busily engaged in painting the front of the Barley Sheaf Inn when one of them slipped from his ladder and fell to the pavement. For some time his workmates tried to bring him round, but without success. "Nip and get some brandy" said one "that ought to do it". "Can't," replied the other "they aren't opened yet". "Well go round the back. Tell them it's an emergency – they won't mind". "That's right," came a voice from the direction of the pavement, "Go on, try the back door!"

Victorian Christmas Cards

A Christmas Tale

THE distant lights were dim through the eyes of John Tregidga as he stumbled along clasping his ragged jacket tight to his frail body, his breathing hoarse in the sharp night air. At twenty eight years old, where already twenty of those years working in wet and filthy conditions underground in the local mines had proved too much, he knew this Christmas would be his last. The distant sound of Christmas Eve bells could be tolling for his funeral. He paused, grateful for the gate to lean on. The mist lay across Halgavor Moor; there was no sound save the bells of St Petroc's ringing out the seasonal message of hope and goodwill. John slowly shrugged his shoulders, goodwill, he still had plenty of that, but hope he had none.

The mine captain had again been turned down his request for a surface job, which although a few pence a week less, may have added a few more months to his life. "No John" he was told "Times are hard, difficult and we can carry no more men on top." Tonight it had taken him an hour to climb the ladders, slippery with slime and water sloshing down from badly maintained pumps. Exhausted, he had slumped down in the drying shed in a desperate effort to recover sufficient energy to stagger home.

"John" a voice burst in on his thoughts, "John Tregidga, come here, man, this is no night for standing brooding." It was Henry Bray, the lay preacher of some renown, a huge figure of a man who, in the moonlight appeared even more greatly enlarged by his winter cape and wide brimmed hat, sitting astride his bow legged donkey, who was as well known for his stubbornness as his owner was for his religious fervour. "You look wisht man, here take my place on the donkey". Before John could reply Henry was off the beast and John seated on. For the next few minutes Henry Bray remonstrated with his donkey using words at times one would not expect to hear from a man of the cloth. Eventually they were on their way, with hymns from the preacher, braying from the donkey and such a hubbub it threatened to make their entry into Bodmin one of complete pandemonium. "John, you must get yourself a h'ass" Henry remarked. "A new pair of lungs would do more good" his companion replied. "Never forget, John, God's ear is waiting for a prayer from you. Tonight get on your knees with fervour, boy and let the good Lord know you haven't forgotten Him". "Another few days, Henry and I will be able to tell Him face to face". John choked on his words and a spasm of coughing left him too weak to talk further.

Henry, a kindly man, led the donkey gently on, his left arm supporting his companion until they reached the miner's cottage in Mill Street. He banged on the door and helped the young man off the donkey. The cottage door opened, a pale faced woman stood in the doorway; her eyes straining in the darkness of the unlit street. "Oh, John" she cried "we have been so worried". "Get him to bed, maid, with some hot broth" boomed Henry Bray's voice around the barely furnished room, causing the four children to shrink back into the shadows.

When Henry Bray left, the family settled down into the now all too familiar evening of children hushed and huddled around the meagre fire, with their father tucked up in bed in an effort to regain his strength for the next day, but even the youngest child knew this could not go on, an air of sorrow and fear for the future pervaded the cottage.

On reaching home, Henry Bray could not dismiss the evening's happenings. He felt the Lord's message this Christmas Eve, now he needed his guidance. Suddenly from prayer he sprang up and grabbed his hat and he dashed from the house to go and knock on street doors; filled with much fervour, as he was to relate on many occasion afterwards. Within the hour his house was all-a-bustle with the kindly folk bearing their promised gifts and by 8 o'clock all was ready. Henry Bray strode forth with his flock behind him.

On reaching Tregidga's cottage all were cautioned to be quiet, then with a downward sweep of the preacher's arm the choir broke out into the first carol. The door flew open and the children peered out. "A Merry Christmas" Henry cried out "May we come in my dears?" The room was swiftly decorated, parcels placed in a corner with strict instructions to the round eyed children not to open until Christmas Day. Food was heaped in the kitchen and logs stacked in the yard. Henry had left nothing to chance.

John was eased up in his bed to partake in a drop of port. "I only drink it for my health, John." said the preacher "It will do you good. Sup up, boy, sup up".

For the family, it was their first real Christmas, a most splendid Christmas, a Christmas beyond their wildest dreams.

For Henry Bray, whose prayer was interrupted by God's guidance, was found rejoicing as he shared the family's Christmas and he silently offered a prayer of thanks.

A happy and peaceful Christmas to One and All.

A Christmas Story

BODMIN Moor lay still; the heavy orange-tinged clouds that had threatened snow all day, now hardly moved, banked up over the high tors. Stock taken down the valley to more sheltered land moved uneasily, sensing bad weather and unhappy with losing freedom, their breath hanging in clouds as they stared in miserable defiance at the farmhouse.

Bosveddar Farm sheltered in the valley bottom, high moorland all around with a grove of beech trees giving some protection from the north winds, snuggled down, windows shuttered and smoke drifting from the chimney. Inside, the Yeo family were getting ready for Christmas. John Yeo and his wife, Morwenna, were moorlanders who went back many generations and had farmed all their married life. For their three children great excitement, not only Christmas Eve, but a first really white Christmas and they could be snowed in as well.

For John though, it was mid-afternoon and he had two hours before dusk, time to saddle his horse and ride out with the dogs for a final check. There were some sheep up near Brown Willy, he might just get them down in time. Pausing in the granite porch, he pulled up his collar. Below the farm he could hear the River Fowey in its infancy gurgling and splashing over rocks eager to be on its way to the sea.

With the two dogs trotting behind he rode away through the field enclosures, then out over the moorland, moving briskly now, sensing the weather changing and knowing only a short time was available. Reaching high ground, he stopped. Over to the west, below old tin workings, he spotted the sheep huddled behind a hedgebank. Sending out the dogs, he watched them swiftly round up and bring the small flock to him. "Twenty, that's all of them," he said thankfully to himself.

Now they had to move quickly, for the light was fading fast and the first snowflakes began to fall. The dogs drove the sheep through a stream, its banks tinkling with icicles as a mournful wind began to increase. Having to climb the high moorland again, he ensured the dogs kept the flock tightly together. On rounding the tor the weather that had threatened all day, broke, snow whirled all around. Now John had to rely on the instinct of the horse to reach the farm; the dogs and sheep had disappeared, around him was a white spiralling wall.

Leaning forward, hat pulled down, his body shrunk in as much as possible, he whispered encouragement to his horse as it slowly plodded forward. The wind now hurled itself against them both, angry that they should disturb its reckless charge across the moor. The snow caught up in this madness drove into their faces, hurting, stinging, burning. Into this insane world, the horse and rider plodded on. Both were now fearful of the moor, the man gave every encouragement to his faithful horse to keep going; it was taking all the generations of moorland living to keep the slender hope he had that they would reach Bosveddar Farm.

Eventually they began to descend steeply, the horse picking its way carefully amongst the granite boulders, gaining shelter in the lee of the tor, giving them a respite from the blizzard. John painfully opened his snow-encrusted eyes and found he was alongside a Cornish hedge. His heart leapt, a hedge of his own enclosures. In the distance he glimpsed the farm's porch lantern swinging to and fro; his horse broke into a tired trot. Behind him he heard a bark and the sound of sheep. On reaching the farm gate his family ran to help him down. The dogs raced the exhausted sheep into the yard, both excited and tired by what had happened.

Later, John sat in an enamel bath in front of the fire, washed himself down, finished the second of two tumblers of brandy and said his prayers, thanking God for the safety of the animals and himself.

Just before midnight the storm cleared. John left his wife by the blazing hearth and made his way through the moonlit snow to the barn. With his arm around the neck of his tired faithful horse, the two loyal dogs at his feet, he gazed up over the barn half-door at the Christmas star and was again moved to offer prayers of thanks that blessed Christmas Eve.

A peaceful Christmas to One and All.

Leskernick Farm, Bodmin Moor ©PD

A Christmas Tale - a truly badgering Christmas Eve

THE boy's dog ran on ahead, leaping from boulder to boulder before disappearing from sight. With a laugh the boy chased after him, happy to be out on such a cold and frosty day after a Sunday morning of hymns and sermons. He stopped, where was Pip? There was no sign of him anywhere. "Pip" he called, "Pip, where are you? Here sir, here boy". Not a sound, where had he gone?

A scuffling noise caused the boy to glance down to a large hole in the bank, a badgers' set. Crouching down on all fours he put his head inside and peered down. A voice called out, making him jump. "Come inside boy if you must and close the door behind you, it's a terrible draught you are causing." Before the boy's wondering gaze in front of a blazing fire stood a large badger, dressed in a red waistcoat, jodhpurs and a tall top hat. The room was well furnished and Badger indicated that the boy should sit in the rocking chair next to the fire, while he pulled up a chair on the opposite side.

Badger lit himself a large cigar, blowing huge puffs of smoke up the chimney. "Well, boy, you were out walking, were you? Strange thing to do during the daytime, prefer the nights myself, would not have got yourself into trouble if it had been night". The boy protested that he had not got himself into trouble; he was just looking for his dog. "Same thing," Badger replied. "Would you have been looking for your dog at night? Of course not, stands to reason". With much puffing and clouds of smoke Badger finished his cigar. "Expect you would like something to eat and drink?" The young lad nodded in agreement; it was lovely and warm in front of the fire. "Good, I will join you." He stood up and shuffled into another room, returning shortly with warm nut muffins oozing with butter and a pot of piping hot acorn tea. "You can't beat acorn tea, keeps a badger lively on his paws, did you know that?" he enquired. "No, I did not," replied his companion, eager to know more about this strange new friend. "Oh yes, whenever I have friends around, which is quite often because I am a very important person in this area of the moor!" As he spoke he was interrupted by an urgent knocking at the door. "Come in, come in, don't stand on ceremony," commanded Badger, eyeing himself in the mirror and adjusting a gold pin in his cravat. The door inched open and two worried looking rabbits peered in. They were dressed in school uniform, green wellingtons and woollen bobbled hats pulled over their ears. "Please sir," the smaller one visibly shook before

Badger's haughty gaze, "Please sir, we have a message to give you from Father Christmas about hay for his reindeer tonight." Badger's face softened; he turned to the boy, "Yes, Christmas Day tomorrow, we always provide refreshments each Christmas Eve on top of the tor, for it's a busy night for Father Christmas. Well done you rabbits, take away a slice of cake each and let everyone know there will be a meeting in the great hall at 5 o'clock to discuss the night's arrangements!" After weedling another slice of cake each the two young rabbits were hustled through the doorway with instructions to "hurry along and no dawdling mind you."

Badger returned to the fire and while pacing up and down explained to his new young friend what would happen that night and how he, Badger, would organise everything. They washed and dried the dishes and after banking up the fire with turf, Badger changed into his outdoor clothes, exchanging his slippers for brightly polished boots and his tall hat for a black bowler. The boy had to admit that he looked very smart indeed. "Quite, quite," said the very important animal, "but I have to keep up appearances; it is expected of me, now, follow behind, no wandering off and getting lost." He picked up a lantern and holding it above his head in one white gloved paw they set off through a maze of tunnels to the great hall.

Before reaching the hall an excited buzz of voices could be heard echoing along the tunnels. On entering, all was suddenly silent. Badger, followed by his companion, made his way to a large chair high on an earthen ledge above the animals. The boy sat behind, enthralled by the whole scene before him. It seemed all the moorland animals were there, some sitting, some standing in the flickering light of the oil lamps set high in the walls of the cave.

Badger held up a white gloved paw for silence. "Friends," he called out, "Friends, we are gathered here because it is Christmas Eve and I have as usual received a message from Father Christmas requesting refreshments." An excited murmur ran through the audience. "So, Major, if you and the horses can see to the hay for the reindeer". The old horse nodded his agreement. "And the rest of you ensure there is plenty for everyone, we will have a jolly good time". An immediate cheer went up, a number of shouts of "good old Badger" started, a chorus of "For he's a jolly good fellow," before he called for silence again. "I will provide Father Christmas with his supper and a drop of acorn tea, hot and strong to help keep out the cold. So, we meet at the Tor at 11 o'clock tonight. Come along boy," said Badger as he pushed his way through the well-wishers, receiving many a slap on the back as he went.

Back in Badger's kitchen a large wicker hamper had been dragged down from the loft to be dusted out and then carefully packed with lots of mince pies, even more nut cake, flasks of acorn tea; serviettes were folded and finally the lid was dropped down and with Badger standing on the top the straps were tightly pulled together.

Badger took out a large gold watch from his waistcoat pocket. "H'm", he mused, "10 o'clock, better get the sledge out; it's been snowing." They made their way outside and down through another tunnel to find a cave full of tools, a sledge and, to the boy's surprise, a bicycle and a kite with a very long piece of string with knots in it. The boy started to ask a question but was interrupted by Badger, "Another time, boy, another time, we have got to load the sledge, time and tide wait for no animal; come along, come along."

Together they heaved and pulled the large sledge to the front door and having got the hamper on the sledge, Badger, with much important huffing and puffing and jangling of keys, locked his front door and they set off, soon to be joined by animals making their way up the Tor. The heavy sledge found many keen helpers to keep it moving to reach the top. Badger was found to be sitting on the hamper so arrived in royal style as befitted such an important animal.

Badger quickly checked on the hay, neatly set out at intervals for the reindeer and supervised the refreshments. All was now set; the excitement was unbearable. Twice Badger had to cuff a young rabbit's ear, who got carried away and hopped across the tablecloth.

The gold watch was checked yet again, "Midnight," he called out "Christmas Day." As the cheers died away reindeer bells could be heard from the direction of the Christmas Star; Father Christmas and his sleigh, loaded up with presents, came into sight. "Hello Badger, good to see you again old friend, a Merry Christmas," greeted Father Christmas and he clasped Badger's shoulders. With hand and paw shaking they made their way to the feast. There was much clinking of mugs and munching of nut cake with icing. Then, Father Christmas called for his reindeer. With much more, sadly all-too-soon paw shaking, cheering, together with lots of reindeer bells tinkling, the heavily laden sleigh took off into the starry sky, for there was still lots more work to do before daybreak.

When all the tea was drunk and all the iced acorn cake munched, the animals joined paws in a circle to sing 'Auld Lang Syne'. Dawn was now breaking and the Christmas Star was low in the sky; it was time to go home. The boy looked around to give Badger a helping hand, but there was no badger. He blinked and looked again; there was just Pip, his dog, up on the bank staring down at him.

Had he been dreaming? The boy looked up at the Tor, no movement save for an old horse slowly making his way down. He stared down near his feet at the entrance to the badgers' set; it sounded like a door being slammed shut and surely wasn't that a trail of acorn cake crumbs?

A Happy and Peaceful Christmas to One and All.

Edwardian Christmas card

A Ghostly Winter's Tale

HOWARD Treven edged a little nearer to the log fire; a small grey haired man who, out of his railway uniform, looked a stranger, although I had always seen him up in his signal box at Bodmin Road station for over the thirty years I had travelled daily from Plymouth to my office. This was a journey I no longer carried out, but today was Christmas Eve and on behalf of my staff I had volunteered to catch an early train to complete documents for signature in order to catch a lunchtime train back to Plymouth. However, on my return to Bodmin General Station I was advised that the lunchtime train had been cancelled due to bad weather and the only one running that day was at three in the afternoon. As the snow was getting worse the railway had arranged for a special goods/passenger train, complete with a snow plough, to come through from Padstow and Wadebridge, the North Cornwall line being completely blocked at Otterham and Delabole. "The George and Dragon inn," the booking office clerk advised, "always has a good blazing fire and is only just down the road, but do not be late back sir, this 'un will be the only train running today."

I had not seen Howard arrive but he looked well settled in the deep armchair by the side of the welcome fire crackling in the hearth. Slowly he put down his glass of ale, inclined his head towards me as if to draw me into his confidence. "It was Christmas Eve," he said, "and had been snowing fit to bust, no transport running, not by road anyways." He paused to light his pipe and sup his ale. "No transport," he repeated, "so I had to walk to Bodmin Road station, three miles, the only way would be to follow the track, leastways what one could see of it. Got on by the Lostwithiel Road Bridge and with the embankment swept dry I thought I would make good time. I set off at a steady pace and looking across the valley towards Lanhydrock I could see smoke curling from farm chimneys. By now 'twas 2.30 in the afternoon, some cold, with a strong easterly wind picking up. No matter, I thought, another hour and I would be in the signal box with a good warm fire. Stopped under the Plymouth road bridge to draw breath, saw in the cutting ahead of me, a great wall of snow with just a narrow track along the line. Still, no worry, no trains on this branch line at Christmas Eve; the weather had seen to that. It was halfway through the cutting, that it happened..." He glanced around nervously as if expecting the landlord to pour scorn on what he was saying, but the landlord was not to be seen ... "You see," he continued, "because of the freezing easterly wind racing up the cutting and the trees bowed down with snow, the narrow track was like a tunnel, that you could just walk upright in. I glanced over my shoulder; the end of the cutting had receded to just a spot of daylight, my stick tapped, tapped the now friendly left hand rail, but how far had I gone, half a mile, one or even two miles? No idea, mustn't panic, so cold, so very cold. Surely not? Suddenly I stopped. No, it can't be, must be hearing things, thought I heard a distant rumble".

He stopped; sweat was forming on his brow. He took a swift draught of his ale, his shaking hand returning the glass to the fireside shelf. "I dropped to me knees," he continued, "put an ear to the rail. Oh no! It was definitely a train approaching, the rail was trembling, the noise getting louder and louder. I scrabbled desperately to dig a hole in the snow to force a way up the side of the cutting. With an almighty roar and a rush it was almost upon me. Terrified by now I only just managed to flatten myself into the hole I had made, as with the most deafening noise and a great whoosh, I was hurled up the bank, hanging on for dear life and this goods train roared on past until the red light of the rocking guards van disappeared in the distance".

With trembling hands he reached again for his ale. "Well, only God in Heaven knows how, I must have clambered back down on the track and made all haste, the train having cleared the snow and soon I could see the very welcome lights of Bodmin Road. I heaved a big sigh of relief on reaching the station, entered the warm signal box. Just couldn't understand it, old Courtney Hancock, my fellow signalman, never recognised me, just got up and muttered something about draught and quickly closed the door. I was in a terrible state, uniform all torn and lost me cap, but it had been terrible cold, the snow you see, the snow."

As the tale ended I gave an involuntary shiver and stared at the empty glass, just as the landlord spoke, "You know, sir," he said as he glanced out of the window, "this weather reminds me of when Howard Treven was found dead in the railway cutting not far from Bodmin Road five years ago, terrible Christmas Eve it was. They ran a special goods train from Padstow/Wadebridge, the North line being blocked you see. They found poor Howard's body the next morning. He'd been thrown up on the bank by the snowplough on the engine. They do say it were the cold that killed him off".

To my question he replied with a worried look "No, sir, you sat on your own by the fireplace all this Christmas Eve lunchtime".

A Happy and Peaceful Christmas to One and All.

A Christmas Tale on Bodmin Moor

FOLLOWING the change of horses at Jamaica Inn on a cold and frosty Christmas Eve the mail coach sped on again towards Bodmin, bouncing and swaying, as the fresh horses pulled hard against the reins, causing the two occupants of the coach to lose their seats and finish in a jumbled heap on the floor. 'Ease back now, ease back' growled the coachman. At the sound of his voice the horses settled back into a trot thus enabling the occupants to regain their seats if not their composure.

'Damn these Cornish highways' complained the small fat man, reaching for his hip flask. 'I swear an oath to God, if he gets me to Bodmin in one piece I will put gold on the church plate'.

'Easy words old friend' said his companion, 'for a gentleman who cannot remember the last time he set foot inside of a church porch'.

'Humbug, humbug' interrupted the small fat man 'it's Christmas Eve, half frozen to death and jolted to kingdom come and back again by a ...' Before he could finish the coach gave a violent lurch to one side and with a startled cry from the guard, toppled off the road with a crash. For a moment, silence, just the spinning of a wheel, then pandemonium. Horses thrashed around, curses from inside the coach, curses from outside the coach as the driver and the guard could justly claim to see more stars at that moment than were rightly in the universe. But slowly things were put to right; the horses were released and the small fat man and his companion recovered from the coach.

'Well master coachman' the small fat man said 'this is a pretty pass, sir, where are we sir? Where are we?'He shivered, the moon lit up the moor but not a light was to be seen from any of the remote farmhouses. They were, he mused, in the middle of nowhere. Devil take the driver, he had battered and bruised him all the way from Launceston, little wonder they should now be looking at an upturned coach.

'We are near Temple, sir, two hours from Bodmin, of course longer if we walk!' Here the coachman was interrupted 'Walk!' exclaimed the small fat man, 'Walk, you throw us from pillar to post then half kill us and now you say we have to walk, no doubt it is safer than travelling with you sir, but walk, no sir, I paid my fare to travel to Bodmin by coach, not by foot, we should have left the coach at Jamaica Inn, should have known it would end like this, you, sir, are an incompetent oaf who should not be in charge of a handcart.'

'All right old friend' his companion said, placing a hand upon his shoulder, 'enough is enough, it's Christmas Eve' he shivered 'now we find shelter, for it's freezing hard'.

With great trepidation the driver offered the information that a small farmhouse stood about a mile back, but we will have to walk there. So they gathered up what could be carried and the sorry group trudged off along an uneven road over Temple Bridge and on up the hill towards the house. The coachman banged on the door; from inside a voice queried what was going on. 'Why 'tis the coachman, my guard and passengers, we've had an accident and require shelter for the night, old friend'.

The bolts were drawn back and the door creaked open. An old farmer peered out 'come in, come in' he cried 'you must be starved to death on a cold night like this. Light the candles Martha, we have guests'. His wife appeared, carrying candles and soon the travellers were huddled around the fire, while the farmer and his good wife were busy in the scullery, and before long mutton and pickles, cheese and bread, glasses of ale and cider were being consumed and a feeling of well-being spread over everyone. Even the small fat man was moved to pat the coachman on the back as he told for the third time the desperate struggle (each time a little more desperate) he put up to keep the coach on the road and how he thought it could have been a wolf not a fox that caused the upset.

From outside the farmhouse door, a soft whinnying could be heard 'Why bless my soul' the coachman cried 'my horses!' Together, with the help of the farmer, the four horses were led into a warm stable, given hay and water, then bedded down for the night with Jed, the farmer's old donkey, seemingly none the worse for their experience.

From the farmhouse the sound of carols now drifted out. 'It's near midnight' said the old farmer leading the way back, and together they joined the others. More furze was thrown on the fire and flames raced up the chimney, more toasts were given and good will radiated all around. The small fat man toasted the coachman and the coachman toasted the small fat man and as they sang carols, out in the stables old Jed led the four horses and cattle facing the angels in the east, to kneel and pay homage to our Lord Jesus at midnight, bringing peace and goodwill all around them on Christmas Day.

A happy and peaceful Christmas to one and all.